I have known Dan Juster fo
life and teaching. I am grat
This important scriptural st
of the Biblical idea of abund ___ ... . abci-
rations of those who teach opulent living for believers and
especially ministers of the Gospel as the biblical norm. It
is geared to build faith in what the Bible really teaches to
empower them walk in a prosperity that promotes in the
spreading of the gospel of the kingdom. I highly recommend it.

—MIKE BICKLE
INTERNATIONAL HOUSE OF PRAYER, KANSAS CITY

Prosperity—What the Bible Really Says is an eye-opening
theological study. With a unique Messianic perspective,
Daniel Juster digs into biblical history and shows how Jesus
handled the topics of wealth and prosperity. If you've ever
wondered what the Bible *really* says about prosperity, this
book is for you.

—ROBERT MORRIS
FOUNDING SENIOR PASTOR, GATEWAY CHURCH
BESTSELLING AUTHOR OF *THE BLESSED LIFE, TRULY FREE,*
AND *FREQUENCY*

As a Pastor and leader in the Church Financial Stewardship
movement I read many books per year about the Bible and
money, but I have not ever read one that lays out an over-
view on prosperity from Genesis to Revelation so clearly
and concisely. Dan Juster's new book, *Prosperity—What the
Bible Really Says* is a must read for anyone desiring to grasp
a complete view of this vital subject. My own understanding
was expanded due to Dr. Juster's passion to diligently understand then teach the Word of God.

—GUNNAR JOHNSON
EXECUTIVE PASTOR, PASTORAL CARE,
EQUIPPING AND DISCIPLESHIP
GATEWAY CHURCH

There are many books written on God's financial provision, but precious few that use the entirety of the Bible in proper context and with sound exegesis. And among those few authors, even fewer have the necessary clarity and faith to both confront the errors and embrace the marvelous realities of God's grace. Daniel Juster has written another masterpiece! *Prosperity—What the Bible Really Says* will not only help many rest their faith safely and firmly on the promises of God and receive from God's unlimited supply, but it is sure to become "standard reading" for anyone studying true biblical prosperity.

—JERRY DIRMANN, SR. PASTOR
THE ROCK, ANAHEIM, CA

Dan Juster is, without a doubt, the preeminent Messianic Jewish theologian of our day. When he writes, it is because he is passionate about the subject matter. His prayerful and thought provoking positions will challenge you from a profoundly studied and balanced place. In our 35 years of walking together I have observed his passion for unity in the Body of Messiah, but that has never eclipsed his pursuit of the truth.

—PAUL WILBUR
PRESIDENT, WILBUR MINISTRIES

PROSPERITY

WHAT THE BIBLE
REALLY SAYS

PROSPERITY

WHAT THE BIBLE
REALLY SAYS

DANIEL JUSTER, THD

Prosperity—What the Bible Really Says by Daniel C. Juster
Published by Creation House
A Charisma Media Company
600 Rinehart Road
Lake Mary, Florida 32746
www.charismamedia.com

Unless otherwise noted, all Scripture quotations are from the New King James Version of the Bible. Copyright © 1979, 1980, 1982 by Thomas Nelson, Inc., publishers. Used by permission.

Scripture quotations marked ESV are from the Holy Bible, English Standard Version, copyright © 2001 by Crossway Bibles, a division of Good News Publisher. Used by permission.

Scripture quotations marked KJV are from the King James Version of the Bible.

Scripture quotations marked NIV are from the Holy Bible, New International Version. Copyright © 1973, 1978, 1984, 2010, 2011, International Bible Society. Used by permission.

Design Director: Justin Evans
Cover design by Judith McKittrick-Wright

Visit the author's website: www.tikkunministries.org.

Library of Congress Cataloging-in-Publication Data:
2016938852
International Standard Book Number: 978-1-62998-544-2
E-book International Standard Book Number:
978-1-62998-545-9

First edition

16 17 18 19 20— 9 8 7 6 5 4 3 2 1
Printed in the United States of America

*God will abundantly provide whatever you
need for whatever you are called to do.*

CONTENTS

Introduction

MY EXPERIENCE ON THIS ISSUE

I WAS A YOUNG undergraduate in 1966 when my friend Thornton announced that he was giving everything away. He had to follow Jesus and live a life of daily faith where he did not own anything. His stereo and other items of value were offered to classmates. He did not give away basic necessities as soap, towels, etc. His parents were still supplying the tuition, room, and board. However, did the Bible really mean for us to give up all private ownership and embrace a vow of poverty?

In 1972 Patty and I were newly married and living in Wheaton, Illinois, near Wheaton College where she was completing her senior year. Two recent graduates asked to visit us with an opportunity. Soon they were presenting a well-rehearsed sales pitch to join Amway, the national products manufacturing, distribution, and multi-level marketing organization.

"What is it you would like to have? A nice vacation in the Caribbean? Perhaps a new model car, or a lovely large house?" The idea was that we could have all our desires if we would join Amway and work hard as distributors. We responded with some astonishment. "Do you realize that you are seeking to recruit us to this business on the basis of material greed and lust? How can you, as Christians, seek to recruit us based on greed?" They were quite taken back, and then replied, "You can use the money however you would like; and, in your case, you can give more money away."

Since that time we were exposed to the faith-prosperity teachers. In 1982 Patty and I attended a conference at Rhema Bible Institute and sat under the teaching of Kenneth Hagin on the Holy Spirit. It was a wonderful time. Patty was amazingly healed of a serious back condition in the adjunct healing meetings. Though Rev. Hagin's topic was not material prosperity, he did say that he had been misunderstood as teaching that all believers were to live in fabulous wealth. He claimed that he was not teaching this; but only if a person builds faith by confessing the Word about God's provision, tithes, and gives generously, that God will lift their material situation. In some cultures it may be a bicycle, others a house to live in. Rev. Hagin stated that provision was applied in various ways in different cultural circumstances. I had no problems with his stated view.

Since that time we discovered why Rev. Hagin was distancing himself from other "faith-prosperity teachers." He spoke against greed and the danger of not dealing with money with integrity. We were also exposed to some televangelists who lived in huge palaces with fleets of cars and seven figure salaries. Some were blatantly over the top in their message on prosperity. One claimed that he was a man of higher faith. Giving to him would produce greater prosperity to the donor than if they gave to a ministry led by men of lesser faith. The proof of their faith was their opulent living. A donor to them could also come into opulent living.

In the mid-90s I met the noted charismatic pastor Jamie Buckingham. He told the story of meeting one of these faith-prosperity teachers. He asked him why he drove a Rolls Royce. The preacher responded that a man in his position needed good reliable transportation. Buckingham noted at a certain point one loses all perspective!

Sometime after this I was the speaker in Barbados for an island-wide conference on "Israel, the Church, and the Last Days." Just prior to the conference one of the faith-prosperity churches on the island sponsored a well-known televangelist. To come he required a $5,000 a night room, a fleet of expensive cars for his contingent, and a very large fee. It was important that the sponsors demonstrate real faith in response to the "man of God." This particular televangelist lives in a large palace-like residence and owns a fleet of Mercedes automobiles. My wife and I stayed in the home of a wealthy couple whose business ventures were a great blessing to the island. Their businesses raised the standard of living for many people. They were very troubled about the meetings of the visiting televangelist and his effect on all the poor people (Barbados has many poor) who were convinced to give their money to the "faith preacher."

Many of the pastors of the island were questioning the teaching and the conference where this preacher was featured. I was asked about my view. I gave a short summary of my views and they were greatly relieved. They also wondered, why is it that so many churches that follow this teaching are independent and do not cooperate with the other churches in the city.

In more recent years, Senator Charles Grassley held hearings to decide if there needs to be greater regulation of churches and religious organizations to stem financial abuse. We have heard of luxury jets, air conditioned dog houses, and very unbalanced overhead percentages in allocating funds given for humanitarian aid. Questions on the separation of church and state have made this a difficult question for the civil government. However, we may eventually find intrusive governmental regulation as a response to financial abuses in the religious non-profit world.

I have attended meetings and churches of Word of Faith preachers. I tire of the constant over emphasis on money. In some churches they there is a weekly mini twenty- to twenty-five-minute sermon on the 1 Corinthians 9 passage on giving before the offering. It is never mentioned that this was a special offering for the poor Messianic Jews of Jerusalem. Yes, we need to teach on generous giving, but a sub sermon every week? In addition many such churches make a high percentage of their main sermons focused on material prosperity. This is imbalanced. I want to make it clear that *not all* who teach prosperity though confessing the Word to build faith present a false teaching that everyone has a right to personal opulence, that as children of the King we should live as kings.

The false teaching has taken root in Brazil where large congregations have been planted under unaccountable leaders who also teach that it is the right of God's children to be rich. It has taken root in Africa. In South Africa one such unaccountable leader, who divorced his wife for a younger woman, just keeps teaching the doctrine of prosperity. Many churches of this orientation are unaccountable to other associations. The head leader is usually unaccountable even in his own church. Elders are mere advisors. They have a dictatorial form of government where, as God's anointed, they are above accountability. In response to this Kenneth Hagin started an association of churches to provide some basic accountability.

Recently an article in the leading Hebrew daily in Israel summarized the teaching and not in a context of it adding credibility to Christianity.

> Under the headline of "Lives of the Rich and Famous," a report in *Haaretz*...noted that Christian leaders are increasingly arguing that Jesus was not poor but rich—an allegation "supported" by the "facts" that he rode on a donkey (ostensibly equivalent in those days to a Cadillac), was given gold at his birth, was well dressed (people fought for his clothes while he was on the cross), and that Judas looked after his funds.[1]

In response to these and other abuses, Rev. Billy Graham and other leaders formed the Evangelical Council of Financial Accountability. They require a real governing board since many of the most abusive ministry leaders have little accountability and have boards composed of their own relatives. The ECFA does not set limits to salaries but does require disclosure that enables donors to see where their dollars are going.

As a Messianic Jew, I am concerned for an accurate Jewish contextual approach to the Bible. What does the Bible really teach in context? The loosely connected Word of Faith movement has produced many books on faith for finances, tithing and giving with the orientation that if you plant seeds of giving they will multiply in financial return. Is this true? The general orientation is toward riches for all. As a leader in the Messianic Jewish movement, I am concerned that our donors do prosper and that we can finance the major projects that are part of our vision. So I am concerned that we get this right.

Others have written on the importance of wealth to

extend the Kingdom of God. Some in the prophetic movement are predicting a great transfer of wealth to the Kingdom of God. However, one leader in this movement in a recent speech said that it seemed that the wealth was transferring to the oil rich Moslem nations and China. Can we expect a wealth transfer? What if the wealth transfer is not to the Western leaders but to the Chinese Christian leaders! The Chinese leaders have lived in great simplicity!

Finally, there are many who still equate spirituality with poverty or at least extremely modest living. They create urban communities, live on a voluntary communal level, and demonstrate God's provision in a context of owning no significant personal wealth. Where do these communities fit into the biblical teaching on wealth? Don't Matthew and Luke quote Yeshua as saying that the poor are blessed? This orientation has a long history in the Church, especially in the monastic movements. Rev. Ron Sider is the most well-known Christian teacher warning against material wealth and steering Christians to modesty in living. Some see an anti-capitalist bent in Rev. Sider's writings. They find this troubling. His writing does seem to reflect a type of Christian socialism.[2]

Strangely, by good management over many years, some monasteries are quite wealthy. I should note in terms of the standards of the Evangelical Council of Financial Accountability, some Catholic parishes and organizations in many nations do not disclose their finances!

I should note that good theology is built from taking into account all the relevant texts to the subject. If there is a selection of texts, they should be representative of the variety of emphases from whole Bible. Most teachers on prosperity are very selective in their use of texts. For example, I have never heard a prosperity teacher, even a balanced one, use 2 Timothy 6 which severely warns against those who teach that godliness is a means of material or financial gain. However, those who teach on simple living seem to think that the Hebrew texts promising prosperity have somehow become irrelevant. This will be the subject of our first chapter.

In researching this subject, I have found little written that is satisfying. There are many books from the faith prosperity school that are almost like boilerplate in repetition. If you have read one, you have read them all. Then there are other writers lambasting Christians as wealthy upper middle class carnal believers because they live in affluence. There are texts from financial advisors that teach Christians to save, invest wisely and give. However, I have found nothing that looks at the primary texts and develops principles that are of universal application for believers today. I do want to see the Kingdom financed. I want to bring some clarity in the midst of the confusion we see today.

Dr. K. P. Yohannan, the great Indian apostle, notes in his writings that much of the money Christians give goes to minimally productive ministries. He argues that amount of gospel progress could be so much greater through giving strategically. It is astonishing. New covenant biblical teaching is not about prospering so "I can get rich" but prospering so I can give abundantly and extend the Kingdom of God. Dr. Yohannan shows us the right attitude for believers in his book *Come, Let's Reach the World.*[3]

I believe that the promise of prosperity in the present stage of new covenant promise and fulfillment is somewhat different than in the pre-new covenant order. We have to make this clear. At the end of our study, I want to have answered three questions.

1. Just **what is the promise of prosperity in this new covenant period?** If we do not correctly understand what the promise is, then we will be believing for something that is not truly promised. One faith teacher said that the new covenant has better promises. This is true, but his conclusion that this means that we are to live in greater riches than promised for the saints in the Old Testament period is questionable.

2. The next and very important question is: **what are the conditions for appropriating the rightly understood promise of prosperity according to today's new covenant order?**

3. **What are the principles for spending money or using wealth in the new covenant order, both for those who live by preaching and teaching the Word and those in other professions?**

PART I

THE BIBLICAL TEACHING ON PROSPERITY

Chapter 1

PROSPERITY AND THE TORAH

A. THE PATRIARCHAL PERIOD

The great German biblical scholar Martin Hengel in his book *Prosperity and Riches in the Early Church* argues that there is no coherent theology in the Bible on this issue.[1] I think that there is an ultimately coherent theology, but only if we realize that the issue of material wealth is complex and is paradoxical. The Bible reflects the paradoxical reality of both the potential blessing of wealth and the dangers.

The patriarch Abraham is our first case study. When God promised that He would bless Abraham, it included material wealth. The text notes that Abraham had significant flocks, servants, gold, and, though delayed for a long time, a growing family. This wealth was a manifestation of God's covenant blessing. Therefore a "faith teacher" might conclude that since we are in covenant with God, we should be wealthy too.

Of course, the wealth of Abraham was in a nomadic context and he would not be considered very wealthy by today's standards! Abraham left his family and probably his inheritance to obey the call of God. There is a significant element of sacrifice and of being a pilgrim in the land that was promised but not yet inherited. There is one reference in the narrative to tithing in the strange and enigmatic text about Abraham giving a tithe to Melchizedek (Gen. 14:18–20). Since he was a priest of God Most High and lived before the Levitical priesthood (Heb. 7:1–11), there may be an interesting implication that tithing is a universal principle and not just something for the Mosaic order. I do think this is the case.

It should be noted that circumstances were not always easy for Abraham. Covenant prosperity includes having children. Abraham lived for many years without having his own children, thus missing this element of prosperity. There were times of famine that were so severe that Abraham traveled to Egypt to survive. So prosperity for Abraham included trials and times where promises were delayed.

In the Book of Genesis, chapters 24 through 50, we read of Abraham's descendants. The narratives concerning Isaac are shorter than for Abraham or Jacob. When Abraham's servant returns to Abraham's ancestors to find a wife for Isaac, he tells the family that Abraham has gained great wealth. This is accepted as a blessing form God. Obviously wealth is not always something to be shunned. Again, there is a setback when Isaac must travel to the land of Gerrar. So life was not always easy.

In the narratives on the life of Jacob, we read of a patriarch whose life was at times prosperous and at times difficult. After escaping from his brother Esau, he worked for his uncle Laban for over twenty years, fourteen of them for his two wives. God supernaturally prospered Laban through Jacob's efforts and in his last period with Laban multiplied Jacob's own flocks so that he would leave Haran with significant wealth. His wealth was primarily in his flock and family, but through such wealth, gold and other precious gems could be acquired. Jacob promised to tithe to God from all that he would receive. Just where this tithe was to be given is not explained in the text. Again, this text is used to show that the tithe to God is a more universal principle and not just tied to the Mosaic order. I agree.

Jacob's life after his return to the land was generally a prosperous nomadic life. However, there were some great trials. The loss of his wife Rachael in giving birth to her son Benjamin was painful. Some think her death was related to her sin of taking the household idols from Laban. Possessing idols opened her to an attack and to death. The idols conferred the right of inheritance. The text does not say that she died due to this sin, but it is possible. The greatest trial for Jacob was the loss of his son Joseph, whom he assumed was dead. Jacob was given the covenant promise of blessing, the promise his descendants would inherit the Land, and certainly God's continued provision. His name was changed to Israel. Yet, before Jacob moved to Egypt to escape famine, he experienced the pain of the famine. No doubt they had to ration their food carefully, but finally did run out of provisions. So it appears that God's blessing did not entail total freedom from apparent setbacks. Setbacks required faith. When Jacob stood before Pharaoh he said that his years were "few and evil" (Gen. 47:9).

Finally, the story of Joseph is one of the great faith stories in the Bible. It certainly shows God's favor on Joseph, but for a significant period, Joseph did not live in great material prosperity. Indeed, he was falsely accused and put in prison. Yes, God was with Joseph and his work in the prison was blessed. Yet years passed without Joseph experiencing a prosperous and free life. Only after he interpreted his dreams to Pharaoh did Joseph rise to prominence in

Egypt. He then rose to a position that included great material wealth, and from that position, saved his family.

In summary

We can see that God's provision was part of the promise of blessing to the patriarchs; but this promise did not preclude trials, some lasting for years, where material prosperity was lacking. There was eventual deliverance, but there were seasons of drought and famine in the land that affected the Patriarchs. Through such seasons God did provide and deliverance eventually came. However, in the case of Joseph the trial was long and difficult. Joseph did not waver in faith.

B. THE MOSAIC PERIOD

The Book of Exodus opens with an account of the people of Israel being enslaved by the Egyptians. I have taught that Israel's period of slavery shows their role as a priestly people who were called to identify and experience the oppression of the peoples on the earth. As for the promise of material prosperity, Israel was led into a long period where the *covenant people* did not experience abundance. The life of these slaves was meager, painful, and dishonoring. This is a great contrast to their future life in the Promised Land. Again I note that Israel had to go through this. God predicted this in revelation to Abraham. We can ask: can believers sometimes be called to trials where material abundance is lacking while yet they are called to have faith in God and believe that it is all for some ultimately good purpose?

Most readers will be familiar with the amazing story of the Exodus. Finally, when Israel leaves Egypt, the Egyptians send them out with significant wealth as a post plague offering. Due to unfaithfulness, the generation of the Exodus died in the desert. Yet they experienced God's provision in manna and quail. Their clothes did not wear out. However, it was a desert wandering existence. Exodus establishes covenant promises for the corporate nation that have an effect on individuals. **Most "faith teachers" do not distinguish corporate promises and individual promises. Doing so helps us to come to better conclusions on just what the Bible is promising.** In Exodus we read that the nation will be prosperous if they obey the covenant. This national prosperity includes promises of health (people will live a full life span without the diseases of Egypt), the elimination of miscarriages, and more (Exod. 15:26; Lev. 26:1–14).

The most astonishing promises of health and prosperity are found in the Book of Deuteronomy or in Jewish parlance, Devarim. We quote the chapter on blessings here, but note that there are repeated shorter texts that have similar promises in the previous chapters.

> Now it shall come to pass, if you diligently obey the voice of the LORD your God, to observe carefully all His commandments which I command you today, that the Lord your God will set you high above all nations of the earth. And all these blessings shall come upon you and overtake you, because you obey the voice of the LORD your God: Blessed shall you be in the city, and blessed shall you be in the country. Blessed shall be the fruit of your body, the produce of your ground and the increase of your herds, the increase of your cattle and the offspring of your flocks. Blessed shall be your basket and your kneading bowl. Blessed shall you be when you come in, and blessed shall you be when you go out. The

LORD will cause your enemies who rise against you to be defeated before your face; they shall come out against you one way and flee before you seven ways. The LORD will command the blessing on you in your storehouses and in all to which you set your hand, and He will bless you in the land which the LORD your God is giving you. The LORD will establish you as a holy people to Himself, just as He has sworn to you, if you keep the commandments of the LORD your God and walk in His ways. Then all peoples of the earth shall see that you are called by the name of the LORD, and they shall be afraid of you. And the LORD will grant you plenty of goods, in the fruit of your body, in the increase of your livestock, and in the produce of your ground, in the land of which the LORD swore to your fathers to give you. The LORD will open to you His good treasure, the heavens, to give the rain to your land in its season, and to bless all the work of your hand. You shall lend to many nations, but you shall not borrow. And the LORD will make you the head and not the tail; you shall be above only, and not be beneath, if you heed the commandments of the LORD your God, which I command you today, and are careful to observe them. So you shall not turn aside from any of the words which I command you this day, to the right or the left, to go after other gods to serve them.

—DEUTERONOMY 28:1–14

First, it is again important to note that the promise is a corporate promise for an ethnic national people. The text is not clear that an individual can appropriate these promises if the corporate people are not faithful. In the Mosaic period, generally, the individual's life is bound to the corporate. The promise to the corporate nation does affect the individual. The text promises regular rains in season, abundance in harvests, growth in flocks, and great population increase. The nation will lend to many nations and not barrow. She will be the head and not the tail. Sickness and poverty will be eliminated. This is all to be fulfilled *if* the nation is loyal to the covenant and obeys its stipulations. Yet, this is an ideal and God also says that there will always be poor people Duet. 15:11).

It should be noted that the Torah provides for caring for the poor by farmers not gleaning the corners of fields (Lev. 23:22) and by exhorting the people to open their hands and give to their people when in need (Deut. 15:8).

The Book of Leviticus, chapter 25, also provides for economic opportunity for all in the context of an agrarian economy. Every fifty years the land is to be returned to their original families of ownership. (In an ultimate sense, God is said to own all the land.) This prevents more and more of the land being owned by fewer and fewer people. The result is greater opportunity for all. In addition, the Torah provides for the cancelation of all debts every seven years. This is the year when lands are to lie fallow and be restored. We see an application of such principles of opportunity in capitalistic societies in modern corporate and personal bankruptcy laws whereby people in debt can get a new start.

The application of the Torah to today, in my view, would lead to the conclusion that any nation that follows the principles of righteousness enshrined in the Bible will see their nation prosper. When the nation prospers, generally the individuals prosper. The teaching that an individual can confess these promises of prosperity and enter into significant material wealth is not clear from the text. There probably is an implication for individuals who live righteously even if the society is unrighteous. Certainly the individual may attain the favor of God in spite of his culture. The extent of such favor on the basis of these texts in regard to material wealth is questionable. We will find other texts of Scripture that do apply righteousness to the ability of individuals to prosper.

Some would say that the United States, as a nation of freedom and righteous law until recent times, has produced great material abundance for its people. Indeed, people on the low middle-class end of the economic ladder are much wealthier than the great majority of people in the world. There is still poverty; but this is not only the result of lack of opportunity, but partly due to deep cultural issues in ghetto cultures. Thomas Sowell, the great African American thinker, has laid out the evidence with great clarity in his book *Race and Culture: A World View.*[2]

While the Torah promises abundant wealth for a covenant faithful nation, it is important to note that that the Ten Commandments include as its last command, "You shall not covet..." (Exod. 20:17). This includes material possessions of any kind owned by a neighbor. There can be abundance without coveting, but coveting is a terrible temptation for human beings. Coveting actually is a great destroyer of prosperity in society.

I think it is fair to conclude that material provision is an implication of the corporate promises to Israel in the Torah. We do not yet have clarity as to any promise of specific levels of opulence for individuals or any promise that there will not be times of material challenge. As the old Scandinavian hymn proclaims, "God has not promised skies always blue, Flower strewn pathways all our lives through."[3]

Chapter 2

PSALMS, PROVERBS, AND PROPHETS

A. PSALMS, PROVERBS, AND JOB

There are numerous proverbs and statements in the Psalms that connect material provision and even significant wealth for the individual who lives righteously. We note a few key ones here.

The writer says that he has never seen the children of the righteous begging for bread (Ps. 37:25). It is declared that "the blessing of the LORD makes rich and he adds no sorrow with it" (Prov. 10:22, ESV). This assumes the ability to gain wealth with integrity. Indeed, of the righteous man we read, "Wealth and riches are in his house, and his righteousness endures forever" (Ps. 112:3, ESV). It is said that it goes well with the man who deals generously and lends and conducts his affairs with justice or righteousness (v. 5). It is not a stretch to say that one could confess such promises before God and ask or expect Him to fulfill His Word. However, this is in the context of loving and believing God and of knowing His personhood and character. These passages give no sense that wealth is bad or dangerous for a righteous man, but they do make it clear that wealth should be used for good.

However, Psalms and Proverbs provide us with another angle on the issue of wealth that is not emphasized in the Torah. For one thing, the text notes that there are wicked people who accumulate great material wealth. The writer of Psalm 73 was very troubled by the prosperity of the wicked but was ultimately comforted in contemplating their end. In addition, they could lose this wealth quickly. He was wrongly tempted to accuse God of injustice in His governing the world. There are several passages where the psalmist cries out to God in the face of the wealthy wicked who oppress the poor and do other works of evil. The poor who are oppressed in the face of evil would be more righteous than the wicked, but the wicked seem to be more materially prosperous. Again there is a very good warning: "He who oppresses the poor to increase his own wealth, or gives to the rich, will only come to poverty" (Prov. 22:16, ESV). Indeed, "a stingy man hastens after wealth and does not know that poverty comes upon him" (28:22, ESV).

In addition, Psalms and Proverbs warn us, as does the Torah, that we are not to put our trust in accumulated possessions, including silver and gold. In fact, it is in the wisdom literature that we find a great warning of danger in wealth as something that can turn us away from God. The writer in Proverbs prays, "Give me neither poverty nor riches, but give me only my daily bread. Otherwise, I may have too much and disown you and say, 'Who is the LORD? Or I may become poor and steal, and so dishonor the name of my God" (Prov. 30:8–9, NIV). The writer seeks a middling state where one has enough but where one does not lose that sense of dependence on God. The greater temptation is in the extremes and the greater safety is in the middle. In my own experience as a pastor, this proverb has often proven to be true. I have never heard a faith-prosperity teacher quote form this text, either orally or in writing.

Proverbs in general repeats the truth that a little with

integrity is much better than great riches and dishonesty. "Better is the little that the righteous has than the abundance of many wicked" (Prov. 37:16). Proverbs even gives us a text that is very applicable today to the most abusive teachers and a warning to those who would follow their teaching. It says that to those who give to the rich to get rich will come to poverty (22:16).

The content of Psalms and Proverbs is therefore more nuanced. There are warnings against the wicked rich. Their wealth is transient. There are clear texts warning against depending on riches. There are texts that declare that wealth can be gained with integrity and is the blessing of God. There are also texts that note the temptation of wealth and even hold up the ideal of a life that is neither rich nor poor.

Job provides us with a corrective to an ironclad doctrine of short-term sowing and reaping. The general tenor can be summarized in a very simple way. Generally Job's friends present the theology of sowing and reaping in terms of the doctrine that the righteous are rewarded with health and wealth. They present this using multiple proverbs and truisms, some profound and some not profound. The conclusion is that Job must have done something wrong to deserve such a terrible plight. Yet, Job professes his innocence. In conclusion, Job is found to be wrong to have accused God of injustice. God has his own good reasons, and in this case it is a test to prove to Satan or all the dark powers that there is such a thing as a righteous loyal man even when it seems that the rewards of righteousness are removed. Even more than this, the Book of Job is probably a cautionary tale against those who would too simplistically apply sowing and reaping in the short term.

Indeed, as the renowned philosopher Immanuel Kant

stated, the rewards and punishments that are due moral behavior can only be ultimately resolved in life after death or the world beyond this.[1] Some years ago, Dr. Michael Brown wrote a fine little book entitled *Compassionate Father or Consuming Fire*[2] on the nature of God in the Hebrew Bible. Part of Dr. Brown's presentation was an evaluation of the thrust on the Book of Job. Job is interpreted in Jewish thought as a special trial. So one must reject the idea that Job, acting in fear, brought his suffering on himself as is taught in the Word of Faith movement. Indeed, though the principles of sowing and reaping are generally fulfilled in this life and the promise of health and provision are trustworthy, they cannot be made absolute in every stage of life. Job lost family, health, and wealth through no fault of his own. Yes, his life and prosperity were restored, but there is no simplistic one-to-one correspondence in this life to wealth, health, and righteousness. Dr. Brown received strong negative reactions to his book from leaders in the Word of Faith movement.

B. The Prophets

In Jewish reckoning, the historical books are counted with the prophetic books. While these books show the same orientation as the prophets in condemning unrighteous gain, including the failure to maintain the principles of debt forgiveness and Jubilee liberation, there is one section of the prophetic-historical books that is of important note—the story of Solomon. The early years of Solomon's reign were years of freedom from external threats, extraordinary trade, and unimaginable wealth. The description of the abundance of gold and silver is astonishing. The whole nation prospered. The early Solomonic period is interpreted in classical Jewish literature as a foreshadowing of the Messianic Age to come. Wealth and great prosperity in Jewish thinking is not evil if it is accepted in a framework of righteousness and care for the needy. This portion of Scripture is part of the framework of Jewish thinking. The early reign of Solomon is a fulfillment of the promise of blessing in Deuteronomy 28.

However, as Deuteronomy warns, wealth can become a source of temptation wherein the person thinks they have gotten it by their own efforts. It can produce self-satisfaction and lack of dependence upon God with a loss of worship and submission. This is what happened in the later reign of Solomon. He lost his zeal for God and entered alliance marriages. He even fostered idolatry. This is why the Davidic period is still seen as a more ideal age. David's kingdom was prosperous but to a lesser degree. With David the faithfulness factor was lasting. The end of Solomon's reign gives us pause and justly leads to ambivalence concerning great wealth.

The prophets continue the more nuanced orientation of the Psalms and Proverbs. They do not condemn wealth *per se.* Yet they understand that a wealthy class has grown up that is not acting justly; is exploiting the workers; and is not living according to Torah standards for generosity, canceling debts, and restoring the land to its ancestral family ownership. The wealthy class has become an evil class. Amos has one of the most famous passages on this matter.

> They hate the one who rebukes in the gate, And they abhor the one who speaks uprightly. Therefore, because you tread down the poor And take grain taxes from him, Though you have built houses of

hewn stone, Yet you shall not dwell in them; You
have planted pleasant vineyards, But you shall not
drink wine from them. For I know your manifold
transgressions And your mighty sins: Afflicting the
just and taking bribes; Diverting the poor from justice at the gate. Therefore the prudent keep silent at
that time, For it is an evil time. Seek good and not
evil, That you may live; So the LORD God of hosts
will be with you, As you have spoken. Hate evil, love
good; Establish justice in the gate. It may be that the
LORD God of hosts Will be gracious to the remnant
of Joseph.

—AMOS 5:10–15

Isaiah 58 is also a very important text.

Is it such a fast that I have chosen? a day for a man
to afflict his soul? is it to bow down his head as a
bulrush, and to spread sackcloth and ashes under
him? wilt thou call this a fast, and an acceptable day
to the LORD? Is not this the fast that I have chosen?
to loose the bands of wickedness, to undo the heavy
burdens, and to let the oppressed go free, and that
ye break every yoke? Is it not to deal thy bread to
the hungry, and that thou bring the poor that are
cast out to thy house? when thou seest the naked,
that thou cover him; and that thou hide not thy-
self from thine own flesh? Then shall thy light break
forth as the morning, and thine health shall spring
forth speedily: and thy righteousness shall go before
thee; the glory of the LORD shall be thy reward.
Then shalt thou call, and the LORD shall answer;
thou shalt cry, and he shall say, Here I am. If thou
take away from the midst of thee the yoke, the put-
ting forth of the finger, and speaking vanity; And

if thou draw out thy soul to the hungry, and satisfy
the afflicted soul; then shall thy light rise in obscu-
rity, and thy darkness be as the noon day: And the
LORD shall guide thee continually, and satisfy thy
soul in drought, and make fat thy bones: and thou
shalt be like a watered garden, and like a spring of
water, whose waters fail not. And they that shall be
of thee shall build the old waste places: thou shalt
raise up the foundations of many generations; and
thou shalt be called, The repairer of the breach, The
restorer of paths to dwell in.

—ISAIAH 58:5–12, KJV

Because of unrighteousness in handling wealth and
injustice in the courts, and because of idolatry, the nation
will be taken into captivity. It is important to note the
constant biblical emphasis on caring for the poor, the
widow, and the stranger. The Bible does not give us an out
by saying that if they are poor or have experienced tragedy,
it must be their fault. If it is a fault of culture, employment
and training can be offered. It is the responsibility of the
members of the society to care for the downtrodden and
to find ways to lift them. The Hebrew Bible makes it clear
that one can be wrongly attached to riches. It can be a
form of idolatry.

The prophet Malachi provides us with important passages on wealth. In chapter 3 we find that the nation is suffering due to many not tithing and lacking generosity. In
addition, we are told that the failure to tithe and bring the
best of the flock for offerings has brought a curse to the
nation. Those who seek to get ahead materially are finding
it slipping away. This is the clearest passage on the rela-
tionship to the tithe in the Mosaic order to God's provision
(vv. 8–12). **If we believe, as I do, that the tithe transcends**

the Mosaic order, then this would have implications for God's provision today. Malachi is basically reaffirming the promises of corporate prosperity in the Torah if the people (and this is an individual decision too) will obey the Torah in tithes and heartfelt devotion to God.

I think it is well to make a few comments on tithing. I have already noted that Abraham gave a tithe to Melchizedek, who foreshadowed the priesthood of Yeshua and the new covenant leadership ministry under Him. In addition, Jacob promised to tithe before the Mosaic Covenant. The tithe in the Mosaic Covenant supported what was their equivalent of the ministry. All Israelites are said to be priests (Exod. 19:6), but a special group was singled out as a priesthood for the Israelites and the world. In the same way, by analogy, the new covenant calls all believers priests but then singles out elders, deacons, and fivefold ministers (Eph. 4:11). This strong analogy is why the historic and Reformation churches have always seen tithing as applicable in the new covenant and a key to God's provision.

SUMMARY OF THE HEBREW BIBLE

The Hebrew Bible generally leads us to conclude that faithfulness to God and His covenant will lead to material prosperity in the nation. This faithfulness includes tithing and generous giving to those in need. Individuals can gain significant wealth and are not condemned for such wealth, but may receive it as a blessing from God. We can conclude that from a Hebrew Bible perspective it is correct to stand on the basis of the covenants for God to fulfill His Word to His faithful people. By the same token, the Bible recognizes that unfaithfulness may well lead to material lack. This is a key theme of Malachi.

Secondly, the Hebrew Bible does provide texts for individual provision. The righteous person is not a beggar and God will meet his needs. In addition, the righteous may well become wealthy by the blessing of God.

Yet the Hebrew Bible makes it quite clear that the wicked may also become wealthy. The unrighteous rich are a constant theme of the prophets. Such wealth will lead to sorrow and can be easily lost.

The Hebrew Bible recognizes that riches may lead to temptation and the writer of Proverbs prays in such a way that it leads to the conclusion that it is best to have provision but to be neither rich or poor. This is the place of the least temptation.

God expects His people to believe His promises as part of affirming His character of goodness. Meditating on the Word and acting on it is already established in the Hebrew Bible as the way toward prosperity. We are to know and believe in God's character of goodness as revealed in the Bible.

Chapter 3

THE TEACHING OF YESHUA-JESUS

HISTORIC CHURCH INTERPRETATION generally presented a picture of Yeshua and His disciples as living a simple life without any significant wealth. The vow of poverty orientation for the most holy has been very strong in both the Catholic and Eastern Orthodox Church. I do want to note a truism that when a person embraces a life without money or possessions, while they cast themselves on God for provision, **this provision comes from those who have money or possessions.** If Yeshua did not own a house, He did stay with people who did. Wealthy women followed Yeshua and gave money for the expenses of Yeshua and His disciples (Luke 8:3). It is interesting to note that if all these women and others who supported Yeshua's ministry gave away all their wealth, it would not have been helpful to the ministry of Yeshua.

Even the person who lives radically by day-to-day provision, even if only by prayer, finds that people who hear the voice of the Spirit give out of their means. People with means are always needed. Judas held the purse for the group. I think it is a misunderstanding to think that a wholesale condemnation of wealth can be derived from the life and teaching of Yeshua. In general, like the Hebrew Scriptures, the teaching of Yeshua provides a paradoxical orientation to wealth.

Yeshua was raised in an artisan's family. He learned the

trade of a carpenter that provided for a modest and adequate lifestyle. It was probably an example of the proverb that calls for neither poverty nor riches (Prov. 30:8–9).

The teaching of Yeshua should be understood in the context of announcing the Kingdom of God. The Kingdom had broken into human history first of all by His presence in first century Israel, then in the circle of His followers. The Kingdom is further in manifestation through the gift of the Spirit at Pentecost and then in bringing the good news of the Kingdom to the nations. The Kingdom has come, but it will not come in fullness until His return. Scholars call this the *already but not yet* understanding of the Kingdom that pervades the Synoptic Gospels.

One of the key aspects for understanding the coming of the Kingdom is a reversal of conditions on earth. I believe that one of the misunderstandings of historical interpretation is in missing the Kingdom reversal dimension in the passage known as the Beatitudes. The historical presentation interpreted the beatitudes as *ways we are to be* to gain God's blessing. People should be poor or at least poor in spirit, meek, and mourning (at least for the sad condition of the world). In the Kingdom view, on the other hand, the listed categories of people are blessed because there is coming a reversal of roles. The poor will no longer be trapped in poverty because the presence and power of the Kingdom enables those who enter it to overcome their poverty. It is a supernatural matter. In the same way, those who mourn are no longer trapped in grief, but are lifted out of it. Those who are meek are no longer the doormats of society but will inherit the earth. Those who hunger and thirst for righteousness will no longer be frustrated but filled. They will experience the righteousness that Yeshua establishes.

The same understanding is reflected in Luke 4 where at the beginning of Yeshua's ministry He quotes Isaiah 61, a text understood as a Jubilee text in the Jewish community. In the year of Jubilee, debts are canceled and lands returned to ancestral families in a massive economic reordering. The trumpet is sounded and liberty is proclaimed throughout the land. So Yeshua proclaims liberty to the captives, the recovery of sight to the blind, and the announcement of the acceptable year of the Lord. In His coming, there is a Jubilee and a reversal of conditions in Israel.

Because the Kingdom has come, the Sermon on the Mount presents a more exacting ethical standard. Easy divorce is precluded. Hatred is rejected, and love for the enemy is enjoined. The issues of the heart are foundational and the motives of the heart are the center of the ethics of Yeshua.

The provision of the Kingdom is so great that one no longer needs to be concerned to store up wealth. Matthew 6:19–24 is a key passage of the teaching of the new covenant on riches.

> Do not lay up for yourselves treasures on earth, where moth and rust destroy and where thieves break in and steal; but lay up for yourselves treasures in heaven, where neither moth nor rust destroys and where thieves do not break in and steal. For where your treasure is, there your heart will be also. The lamp of the body is the eye. If therefore your eye is good, your whole body will be full of light. But if your eye is bad, your whole body will be full of darkness. If therefore the light that is in you is darkness, how great *is* that darkness! No one can serve two masters; for either he will hate

the one and love the other, or else he will be loyal
to the one and despise the other. You cannot serve
God and mammon.
                                        —MATTHEW 6:19–24

What does it mean to not "lay up" for ourselves treasures on earth? At least on the face of it, it is difficult to
see how the personal ownership of great wealth is consistent with this passage. Gold, silver, jewelry, and real
estate—farmland and houses—constituted treasures on
earth in those days and these are treasures on earth today.
In addition, bank accounts and stocks and bonds consti-
tute treasures on earth today. The text says that such treasures are transitory. "Moth and rust" will corrupt them.
Rather we are to lay up treasures in heaven. This is not
a new doctrine, but in Jewish thought good deeds follow
the faithful to their life after death. It provides everlasting
enrichments or treasures in heaven.

In addition, if one is motivated by greed, that is if the
eye is evil, one is filled with darkness. One cannot serve
God and material wealth (mammon).

These are strong warnings and do give support to those
who call upon all believers to live a simple life. However,
the text does not preclude accumulating wealth to do good
deeds for others. The text does bring into question the
righteousness, in present stage of new covenant Kingdom
order, of living in great opulence.

We should add to these texts the parable of the talents
(Matt. 25:14–18). This was an amount of money that was
given to the servants for trade. The one servant that did
not trade successfully, but hid the talent in the ground
and then returned it, was rebuked. This one talent was
removed from his stewardship and given to another. The

faithful servants are rewarded with the rulership of towns. It should be noted that the text is a parable. It is not a literal teaching on expanding wealth. However, it can be applied in that God expects us to use all we are given to expand the Kingdom of God and that could imply a wise use of wealth. Could some be called to multiply wealth to extend the Kingdom of God?

One of the most beautiful texts of Scripture then teaches us to not depend on possessions. If we trust in God and live in and from the Kingdom, God will provide for all our needs. We therefore are to be free from worry and concern for accumulating material possessions. Yeshua said,

> Therefore I say to you, do not worry about your life, what you will eat or what you will drink; nor about your body, what you will put on. Is not life more than food and the body more than clothing? Look at the birds of the air, for they neither sow nor reap nor gather into barns; yet your heavenly Father feeds them. Are you not of more value than they? Which of you by worrying can add one cubit to his stature? So why do you worry about clothing? Consider the lilies of the field, how they grow: they neither toil nor spin; and yet I say to you that even Solomon in all his glory was not arrayed like one of these. Now if God so clothes the grass of the field, which today is, and tomorrow is thrown into the oven, will He not much more clothe you, O you of little faith? Therefore do not worry, saying, "What shall we eat?" or "What shall we drink?" or "What shall we wear?" For after all these things the Gentiles seek. For your heavenly Father knows that you need all these things. But seek first the kingdom of God and His righteousness, and all these things

shall be added to you. Therefore do not worry about
tomorrow, for tomorrow will worry about its own
things. Sufficient for the day is its own trouble.

—MATTHEW 6:25–34

Asher Intrater, my disciple from 1978 and my colleague
since that time, has well said that true wealth is like a
carpenter not having to carry a large tool box. Whenever
he needs the tool, it appears in his hand. Those who are
called to live totally by faith and prayer with no substance
to carry around, live in a particular kind of blessedness. In
the new order of the Kingdom brought by Yeshua, holding
personal possessions are not necessary for a disciple's provision. The text does not, in my view, preclude that one
may be called to handle great wealth for the Kingdom. **The
key is that all are called to a worry free life with regard
to material provisions.** All are to seek the Kingdom of
God first so that all one's needs may be met. This means
that God's provision is based on more than just confessing
biblical passages, as good as this is. It is based on a whole
heart orientation to the Kingdom of God, loving God, and
seeking to extend His Kingdom in all the ways to which
He calls us.

The Gospel of Luke, chapter 6, adds to our theology of
material wealth by enjoining generosity.

> Give, and it will be given to you: good measure,
> pressed down, shaken together, and running over
> will be put into your bosom. For with the same mea-
> sure that you use, it will be measured back to you.
>
> —LUKE 6:38

Abundant provision from God is thus based on giving
generously. This takes faith in God and His promises. The

history of the apostles shows us that this does not imply a right to live in opulent wealth. All of them lived simply. However, those who are called to handle wealth for the Kingdom may gain the ability to handle even more wealth for the Kingdom if they maintain their faith-generosity way of life. Those with modest means still will find that faith-generosity produces abundant provision even if not opulent living.

In addition, we find a challenge to the wealthy in the passage on the rich young ruler.

> Now as He was going out on the road, one came running, knelt before Him, and asked Him, "Good Teacher, what shall I do that I may inherit eternal life?" So Jesus said to him, "Why do you call Me good? No one is good but One, that is, God. You know the commandments: 'Do not commit adultery,' 'Do not murder,' 'Do not steal,' 'Do not bear false witness,' 'Do not defraud,' 'Honor your father and your mother.'" And he answered and said to Him, "Teacher, all these things I have kept from my youth." Then Jesus, looking at him, loved him, and said to him, "One thing you lack: Go your way, sell whatever you have and give to the poor, and you will have treasure in heaven; and come, take up the cross, and follow Me." But he was sad at this word, and went away sorrowful, for he had great possessions. Then Jesus looked around and said to His disciples, "How hard it is for those who have riches to enter the kingdom of God!" And the disciples were astonished at His words. But Jesus answered again and said to them, "Children, how hard it is for those who trust in riches to enter the kingdom of God! It is easier for a camel to go through the eye of a needle than for a rich man to enter the

kingdom of God." And they were greatly astonished, saying among themselves, "Who then can be saved?" But Jesus looked at them and said, "With men it is impossible, but not with God; for with God all things are possible."

—MARK 10:23–27

The rich young ruler is challenged to give away his wealth and to follow Yeshua. He leaves with sadness. He is unable to pass the test. Yeshua then teaches that it is harder for a camel to go through a needle than for a rich man to enter the Kingdom of God. The disciples, who identified wealth (at least sometimes) with the blessing of God, wonder who then can be saved. Yeshua responds that with God all things are possible.

How shall we interpret this passage? Is Yeshua saying that the rich have to give away all their riches to enter the Kingdom, and that this is hard for them to do? Or is He only saying that the rich find it very difficult to have a right heart attitude to their possessions, and this is necessary to attain to entering the Kingdom of God. Yeshua did **not** say that one cannot be rich and be in the Kingdom of God, but that it would be difficult for rich people to enter it. The Luken version of the Sermon on the Mount, sometimes called the Sermon on the Plain, does include woes upon the unrighteous rich (Luke 6:24–25). This fits a general pattern of teaching in Luke wherein Jesus gives serious warnings to the unrighteous wealthy. In the story about the rich man and Lazarus, the rich man ends up in hell and Lazarus, the poor leper, in Paradise (16:19–31). The rich man refused to use his wealth for the benefit of the needy. In addition, the rich man, who stored up crops and built barns to secure his future, dies and all his efforts come to nothing (12:13–21). The context of this passage is telling. Before the passage we read a warning that a man's life does not consist in his abundance of possessions. After it we read the parallel to the passage in Matthew 6 where we are taught to not worry about financial provision but to consider God's provision for the birds and His dressing the grass of the fields. We quote Luke in context.

> Then one from the crowd said to Him, "Teacher, tell my brother to divide the inheritance with me." But He said to him, "Man, who made Me a judge or an arbitrator over you?" And He said to them, "Take heed and beware of covetousness, for one's life does not consist in the abundance of the things he possesses." Then He spoke a parable to them, saying: "The ground of a certain rich man yielded plentifully. And he thought within himself, saying, 'What shall I do, since I have no room to store my crops?' So he said, 'I will do this: I will pull down my barns and build greater, and there I will store all my crops and my goods. And I will say to my soul, "Soul, you have many goods laid up for many years; take your ease; eat, drink, and be merry."' But God said to him, 'Fool! This night your soul will be required of you; then whose will those things be which you have provided?' "So is he who lays up treasure for himself, and is not rich toward God."
>
> —LUKE 12:13–21

After the passage on trusting God for provision, Yeshua adds the following,

> Do not fear, little flock, for it is your Father's good pleasure to give you the kingdom. Sell what you have and give alms; provide yourselves money bags which do not grow old, a treasure in the heavens

that does not fail, where no thief approaches nor moth destroys. For where your treasure is, there your heart will be also.

—LUKE 12:32–34

When we look at the whole of the text on riches in Luke 12, we again see more of a warning against trusting in wealth though His immediate disciples are to sell what they have. This is the strongest passage where one could make a case that all disciples are to live the simple life, to pay their way from what God provides, and to renounce wealth and ownership. However, I think that this conclusion goes too far. I think that this is a specialized situation for those who were in the core group of Yeshua's disciples and were following Him around the country and part of His ministry. This was how they were to live. It has to be balanced with other passages. The passage does give an endorsement to the idea that some are called to this simple life of faith provision.

We should note the other passages where Yeshua did not require all the wealthy to give away all their wealth. The wealthy women who supplied His needs were not called to give up their wealth. In addition, when Zacchaeus professed that he would give *half* of his wealth to the poor, Yeshua stated that the Kingdom had come to Him. Yeshua did not respond and say that he needed to give *all* his wealth to the poor. His instruction to Zacchaeus was different than that given to the rich young ruler. There were wealthy supporters in addition to the women. Joseph of Arimathea is a wealthy man who provided for the burial of Yeshua. Nicodemus, who was also a man of wealth, was not told to give up his wealth as a condition of being born again. So the passage on the rich young man is situation specific and cannot be used as a proof text that Yeshua's disciples should have no possessions.

We finally note that Yeshua and His disciples lived a life that was very free from material possessions. Those who try to find the opposite because Yeshua had an expensive seamless robe and assert that the treasury maintained by Judas was a very lucrative treasury are offering very silly arguments with no textual basis. They plead for such interpretations to defend an opulent lifestyle.

Indeed, Yeshua provides us with an example of a person who serves God with no significant ownership of wealth. He has no home of His own!

> And Jesus said to him, "Foxes have holes and birds of
> the air have nests, but the Son of Man has nowhere
> to lay His head."
> —LUKE 9:58

The disciples enter into this simple life. They are to go from city to city expecting provision from those they serve. They do not take extra clothes or money (Luke 9:3). This was an example for all of those who have sensed a call from God to live totally by faith without significant personal possessions. George Mueller in nineteenth-century England provided for thousands of children in his orphanages but had no personal ownership of significant wealth and left this earth without leaving any wealth to his descendants. Hudson Taylor, the great Protestant missionary to China lived a similar life. Peter could say at Pentecost, "Silver and gold have I none" (Acts 3:6, KJV).

In summary

The Gospels do not provide an overall philosophy of wealth but leave us with some guidelines. We are not to "lay up" for ourselves treasures on earth. We are to trust in God's provision. We are to note the dangers of depending on our possessions, for this can prevent people from entering into and living from the Kingdom of God. On the other hand, wealthy people are accepted by Yeshua and are not always called to give away all their possessions. In addition, generous giving will lead to a significant increase for wealth management. Peter notes that in contrast to the rich young ruler, they have left all to follow Yeshua. Yeshua states that they will be given much more in return, even a hundredfold in friendship and houses in this life and in the fullest life in the age to come (Matt. 19:27–30). (They are not told they will own these houses, but they will find they will be provided with such houses.)

We are to make friends with unrighteous mammon (material possessions or money). Then they will receive us into internal habitations. The Gospels tend to be much more oriented to warning against at the wrong orientation toward wealth than encouraging us to acquire it for the right use. There is no encouragement to its accumulation for personal living. In addition, the judgment of God is connected to how we deal with the needy. Matthew 25:31–46 shows the great judgment in terms of how we feed and clothe those in need, the least of His brethren (v. 40). Some see the reference to brethren as referring to disciples of Yeshua, some to Jewish people, and some to the human race.

Chapter 4

ACTS, THE PAULINE EPISTLES, AND MORE

A. THE BOOK OF ACTS

The Book of Acts provides some interesting material for our reflection. First of all, the community that forms after the outpouring of the Spirit manifests a high degree of egalitarian sharing. The text says that the believers had all things in common. Many have taken this to mean that the community was socialistic and lived from a common pot. The wealth was in the hands of the apostles. Exactly how this was done we are not told, nor how the homes of the believers could be held in common. Others have pointed out the possibility that the Jerusalem community was not socialistic; but that in heart all considered all they had to be for the sake of all, and they would sell their possessions as others had need.

The story of Ananias and Sapphira is considered a proof of that. Peter told them that before they sold their property it was theirs to use as they desired (Acts 5:4). Apparently there was no requirement to sell all to be a member of the community. Their issue was lying to the community; which, as the place of the manifestation of the Holy Spirit, required holy and truthful living. Both died as a result.

The Jerusalem community prospered, and we are told that no one was in need (Acts 4:34). There were issues of

31

fair distribution for those who needed support, but that was solved by the choosing of deacons in Acts 6. They would oversee fair distribution.

By the end of the Book of Acts, the Jerusalem community had undergone great change. A persecution had taken place that scattered most of the apostles. James (Jacob) remains. In addition, there was a major regional famine. The Jerusalem community became a community with many in serious need. To meet this need, Paul received offerings from his diaspora congregations. The offering for the Jerusalem saints had two primary purposes. One was to show unity with the Israeli branch of the body of believers, and the other was to meet the needs of the original community that had established the new covenant Kingdom on the earth.

Paul did not accumulate wealth. He was supported by tent making and sometimes by offerings. Generally, he lived by his tent making since **he did not want anyone to think that he used the gospel to make a profit**. In this way he was not indebted to donors (1 Cor. 9:7–18). The Epistles reinforce this picture. Paul did not reject wealthy people. Some government officials and wealthy people did respond to the gospel. There is no passage in his writings or account in the Book of Acts where believers were told to give away all their wealth as a condition for membership in the community. In some cities wealthier people who had already been connected to the synagogue responded to the gospel.

However, Paul does make it clear in his epistles that this was a minority. In 1 Corinthians 1:26, he says, "Not many were influential; not many were of noble birth" (NIV); but this implies that some were. Also those who met in houses needed a good amount of space. The houses probably were provided by wealthier members. Those who responded in Corinth who were leaders of the synagogue would have had wealth. Those who responded in Acts were sometimes wealthy.

The Book of Acts provides us with an implied life orientation. As the apostles came to the realization of the meaning of Yeshua's command to disciple the nations, resources were committed this goal. This included great personal effort as well as material support. The implications of the Great Commission of Matthew 28 will be a key in our developing a new covenant orientation to wealth.

B. The Pauline Epistles

The example of Paul in the Book of Acts is consistent with his profession in his writings. He shows little concern with wealth. He expected God to provide by his profession and by contributions. In general, he depended on his profession. However, he clearly taught that those who preach and teach in the body of believers were worthy of double honor or good pay (1 Cor. 9:7-19; 1 Tim. 5:17-18). The idea of paid ministers was fully accepted.

When Paul speaks about his own life, the issue is to do whatever it takes to be faithful to his calling and to do all he can to extend the Kingdom of God. In this he tells us that he learned to abound and to be abased.

> Not that I speak in regard to need, for I have learned in whatever state I am, to be content: I know how to be abased, and I know how to abound. Everywhere and in all things I have learned both to be full and to be hungry, both to abound and to

suffer need. I can do all things through Christ who
strengthens me.

—PHILIPPIANS 4:11–13

There were times of imprisonment and beating. There
were times of abounding material blessing in the homes
of those who supported the work. Paul did not accumulate material wealth. However, he does give important
teaching about riches.

Second Corinthians 9 and Romans 15 provide two very
important passages on the issue of wealth. The first is a
primary text for the "prosperity gospel" teachers. The context of both passages is Paul's taking up offerings for the
Jerusalem believers who had become needy. According
to the Romans passage, this is a duty. Since the Jewish
believers brought the gospel to the Gentiles, thus the
Gentiles are forever in the debt of the Jews. In this regard,
they who have been partakers of the spiritual blessings of
the Jews are to offer them material blessing and support
in their time of need (Rom. 15:26–27). Romans tells us to
avoid debt and to owe nothing to others but to love one
another (13:8).

The 2 Corinthians 9 passage adds a context to the
teaching on the nature of giving and prosperity. We quote
this passage in full since it is such a key passage.

> Now concerning the ministering to the saints, it
> is superfluous for me to write to you; for I know
> your willingness, about which I boast of you to the
> Macedonians, that Achaia was ready a year ago; and
> your zeal has stirred up the majority. Yet I have sent
> the brethren, lest our boasting of you should be in
> vain in this respect, that, as I said, you may be ready;
> lest if some Macedonians come with me and find

you unprepared, we (not to mention you!) should be ashamed of this confident boasting. Therefore I thought it necessary to exhort the brethren to go to you ahead of time, and prepare your generous gift beforehand, which you had previously promised, that it may be ready as a matter of generosity and not as a grudging obligation. But this I say: He who sows sparingly will also reap sparingly, and he who sows bountifully will also reap bountifully. So let each one give as he purposes in his heart, not grudgingly or of necessity; for God loves a cheerful giver. And God is able to make all grace abound toward you, that you, always having all sufficiency in all things, may have an abundance for every good work. As it is written: "He has dispersed abroad, He has given to the poor; His righteousness endures forever." Now may He who supplies seed to the sower, and bread for food, supply and multiply the seed you have sown and increase the fruits of your righteousness, while you are enriched in everything for all liberality, which causes thanksgiving through us to God. For the administration of this service not only supplies the needs of the saints, but also is abounding through many thanksgivings to God, while, through the proof of this ministry, they glorify God for the obedience of your confession to the gospel of Christ, and for your liberal sharing with them and all men, and by their prayer for you, who long for you because of the exceeding grace of God in you. Thanks be to God for His indescribable gift!
—2 CORINTHIANS 9:1–15

There are several important principles to note in this passage. First, people are to give willingly. This means that attaining a generous orientation to our wealth is central to giving and new covenant Yeshua-like character. Parallel to Luke 6, Paul teaches that generous giving brings a multiplication of wealth back to the giver. It is like sowing seed. The seed that is sown comes back as a crop of countless seeds. If we sow generously, we will reap generously. This passage has been the foundation of the teaching of the "prosperity gospel" leaders that the way to wealth is through generous giving and that this passage and others should be confessed or recited to build faith. It should be pointed out that Paul is probably not teaching a mathematical formula for multiplying material wealth. One's generous giving from a generous heart will over the long haul bring great blessing in return, but such blessing should not be measured in material things alone. The whole of life in all dimensions is enhanced for a generous person. On the other hand, generous giving provides the probability of God's entrusting the giver with more wealth to allocate. Generous people desire to expand their ability to give more, and God often meets that desire. As Proverbs says,

> There is one who scatters, yet increases more; And there is one who withholds more than is right, But it leads to poverty.
> —Proverbs 11:24

The 2 Corinthians passage along with Luke 6 are the two key New Testament passages that imply wealth multiplication though generosity. However, there must be a love motive for giving. Paradoxically, if the person is giving for the sake of getting for self, the principle is non-operative. This is very clear in the Corinthian passage where Paul teachers about the nature of the liberal heart of giving as a godly way of living.

I think it is well to note that these offerings assume that people have money to give, whether savings or possessions they can sell. It was not characteristic of Paul's communities that all gave up all of their possessions to serve the Kingdom.

In another context Paul encourages godly living and generous giving, in this case supporting Paul in his need. He states, "And my God shall supply all your need according to His riches in glory by [Messiah] Jesus" (Phil. 4:19). The key to God's provision again is generous giving and serving the gospel.

The Pauline writings are also quite clear on the dangers of riches. As Paul demonstrates, it is a legitimate call to forgo personal possessions. He is very concerned to show that he does not profit from preaching the gospel. Though ministers can legitimately be well paid, there is a line that must not be crossed or it discredits the ministry. **This line is giving the world opportunity to criticize the minister as preaching the gospel because they are in it for the money.** In this regard, Paul's strongest warning is in 1 Timothy 6:5–10, a passage I have never heard quoted by "prosperity gospel" teachers,

> who suppose that godliness is a means of gain. From such withdraw yourself. Now godliness with contentment is great gain. For we brought nothing into this world, and it is certain we can carry nothing out. And having food and clothing, with these we shall be content. But those who desire to be rich fall into temptation and a snare, and into many foolish and harmful lusts which drown men in destruction and perdition. For the love of money is a root of all kinds of evil, for which some have strayed from the

faith in their greediness, and pierced themselves
through with many sorrows.

Paul rips into those who would hold that godliness is
a means of financial gain. In addition, he says that those
who desire to be rich fall into many temptations. Some
have made a shipwreck of their faith by yielding to such
desire. No doubt those who have done so gave good spiri-
tualization for their use of the gospel as means to enrich
themselves. How many religious personalities have done
just this! They have told the gullible that by making them
rich they would also get rich! Truly "the love of money is
a root of all kinds of evil." (We indeed see such false love
as a root of evil enterprises from pornography to prostitu-
tion, to slave labor, and to unfair labor practices. It is the
root of gambling. It is one of the greatest dangers to our
souls.) Hebrews 13:5 states, "Let your conduct be without
covetousness; be content with such things as you have. For
He Himself has said, 'I will never leave you nor forsake
you.'" The NIV is also worth quoting here, "Keep your
lives free from the love of money, and be content with
what you have."

In 1 Timothy 6 Paul gives instruction to the rich. It is
not that they are to give away all their wealth.

> Command those who are rich in this present age not
> to be haughty, nor to trust in uncertain riches but
> in the living God, who gives us richly all things to
> enjoy. Let them do good, that they be rich in good
> works, ready to give, willing to share, storing up for
> themselves a good foundation for the time to come,
> that they may lay hold on eternal life.
>
> —1 TIMOTHY 6:17–19

This passage is a key passage of guidance for wealthy people. Paul even states that God gives us richly all things to enjoy. Those who have no great possessions can enjoy much! However, the rich can also enjoy that which God gives richly for our enjoyment. This is no council of poverty or asceticism. However, the main thrust is that the rich are to use their wealth for good works, to give and to share.

There is one more important teaching on material wealth. This is especially found in the Timothy and Thessalonian correspondence. The community is to take care of those with legitimate needs, especially true widows. This is a corollary of love. However, they are to not give to those who are lazy and do not seek to provide for themselves. The other corollary of love is that the member will not seek to be a burden on the community. In regard to love, children are to provide for their parents when they are in need, and to not do so makes them worse than infidels. Personal responsibility for one's provision is a strong teaching in these epistles. (See 1 Timothy 5:3–11 and 2 Thessalonians 3:6–15.) These passages assume that people work diligently and accumulate sufficient provisions to provide for their families. Instructions for heads of families is different than for unmarried disciples who can travel with an itinerate minister. The greater freedom of the unmarried to serve the gospel is Paul's preferred way of life in 1 Corinthians 7.

The great conclusion from Acts and Paul is that a simple life is valued. The use of the gospel to get rich is forbidden. The principle of abundant provision is taught as based on generous faith-giving. We are to care for fellow believers who are in true need, but also hold people responsible to seek to provide for themselves. Wealthy people are called to use their wealth to extend the gospel and to care for those who are in need. Those who have much are to share with those who have little. There is no general teaching that the wealthy are to give up all their wealth like the rich young ruler.

C. The General Epistles and Revelation

The most significant writing on riches in the General Epistles comes from the Book of James. This epistle parallels other Jewish ethical teachings and warns severely against the ungodly use of wealth. James warns the rich to not depend on their riches, and commands them to use their riches for the good of others. They are to wail in repentance over the misuse of wealth. In addition, he severely warns congregations to not show favoritism to the rich, because as a class, they were oppressing others. When the congregation gathers, they are not to be singled out for special treatment and given the best seats. Yet, significantly, James does not tell the rich to give away all their riches. The texts of the Book of James are well worth quoting.

> My brethren, do not hold the faith of our Lord
> Jesus Christ, the Lord of glory, with partiality. For
> if there should come into your assembly a man with
> gold rings, in fine apparel, and there should also
> come in a poor man in filthy clothes, and you pay
> attention to the one wearing the fine clothes and
> say to him, "You sit here in a good place," and say
> to the poor man, "You stand there," or, "Sit here at
> my footstool," have you not shown partiality among
> yourselves, and become judges with evil thoughts?

Listen, my beloved brethren: Has God not chosen
the poor of this world to be rich in faith and heirs
of the kingdom which He promised to those who
love Him? But you have dishonored the poor man.
Do not the rich oppress you and drag you into the
courts? Do they not blaspheme that noble name by
which you are called?

—JAMES 2:1–7

Come now, you rich, weep and howl for your mis-
eries that are coming upon you! Your riches are cor-
rupted, and your garments are moth-eaten. Your
gold and silver are corroded, and their corrosion
will be a witness against you and will eat your flesh
like fire. You have heaped up treasure in the last
days. Indeed the wages of the laborers who mowed
your fields, which you kept back by fraud, cry out;
and the cries of the reapers have reached the ears of
the Lord of Sabaoth. You have lived on the earth in
pleasure and luxury; you have fattened your hearts
as in a day of slaughter. You have condemned, you
have murdered the just; he does not resist you.

—JAMES 5:1–6

One cannot read the whole Bible and think that if James
is in accord with it, that he is condemning all wealthy
people. However, his writing fits the historic prophetic
stream of condemnation for the unrighteous wealthy. So
why does James not make the distinction more clearly as
it is made in the Hebrew Bible. It is because at his time,
and the evidence of history supports this view, the level
of corruption in society was such that the rich class, as
they impacted the Jewish community, was an unrighteous wealthy class. Of course there were exceptions. As
we before stated, Paul in 1 Timothy 6:17–18 told Timothy

to tell the rich to use their wealth for good works. This is parallel to James. Neither told the wealthy not to give away all their wealth.

The Book of Revelation does have implications for the issue of wealth. It does not teach us about the individual's responsibility in the use of wealth. Rather it presents us with an economic and social system where the system of the supply of goods and trade are controlled by an evil system that requires people to worship the Antichrist. This is the Babylon system.

For us, compromise with evil for the sake of material gain or even provision is forbidden. This implies that wealth much be attained by honest motives and means. I am reminded of an investment newsletter that has what it calls a "sin portfolio." This portfolio has weathered the recent economic downturn and has outperformed many mutual funds and other stock allocation plans. No follower of Yeshua could invest in its stocks that include tobacco companies, gambling concerns, and pornographic magazines!

To yield to evil for the sake of material gain, to accept the mark of the beast, and to embrace the Babylon system will lead to eternal loss.

Chapter 5

CONCLUSIONS ON BIBLICAL TEACHING

THE HEBREW SCRIPTURE emphasis is mostly on the principle that the corporate covenant faithfulness of the nation will lead to corporate national blessing which includes great material wealth. Individuals will participate in the blessings of such wealth. In addition, there are individual promises that generosity and honesty in business will lead to prosperity for the individual. Poverty is never idealized. The Patriarchs and the early reign of Solomon largely show the fulfillment of the promise of material blessing in the context of righteousness.

However, the Hebrew texts present another side. There are many texts that warn against unrighteous gain and evil behavior by a rich class that oppresses the rest of the population. This is a pervasive theme of the prophets. Justice does include economic opportunity as enshrined in the forgiveness of debt on the Sabbatical year and a new start in the Jubilee year. Justice includes fair wages for the employed. Generosity for the widow, the orphan, and the stranger are repeatedly emphasized. In addition there are warnings about selfishness and coveting. The one who withholds may come to poverty, but the generous righteous man will not beg bread.

However, the promise does not mean that there is an airtight case for an easy life. There are reversals at times for Jacob, Joseph, and Job. In addition, there is a strong warning on the danger of depending on riches and becoming self-sufficient. The ideal of a balance or a medium between poverty and riches is put forth by the writer of Proverbs.

Tithing in the Hebrew Bible is a foundation for financial security. The idea of tithing is first revealed in the Patriarchal narratives and is codified in the Mosaic legislation. The tithe supports the Levites and the priests. In addition, the animal offerings brought to the temple must be without blemish or it will affect one's prosperity.

In the New Covenant Scriptures, in contrast to the Hebrew Scriptures, there is greater emphasis in warning against ungodly gain and the dangers of wealth. However, this does not mean that the new covenant departs from the idea of God's abundant provision. Indeed, the sense of these texts is that God will respond to the law of sowing and reaping. There will be abundant provision for those who walk in covenant faithfulness and obey the law of sowing and reaping. In this regard, the one who sows generously cannot out give God, but God will respond to this person with generously. **The way to prosperity is in covenant faithfulness, integrity, and generous giving. One can confess and stand on the promise of God's abundant provision according to Philippians 4:19.** This abundance is in a context of supernatural provision where disciples are called to not store up treasures on earth for where one's treasure is, there will one's heart be (Matt. 6:21; Luke 12:34). In addition, the idea that the preaching of the gospel is a means of financial gain is severely condemned (1 Tim. 6). Ministers must not get rich on the gospel. On the other hand, the New Testament never gives a general command for the rich to give away their wealth and become formerly rich.

The Gospels and the example of the apostles do give examples of forsaking wealth and trusting in God's provision by faith. Ministers can live by people supplying their needs. This is a life of simplicity. A life of abandoning wealth and living by faith is a legitimate biblical calling.

The idea of abundant provision has to be balanced by the call to sacrifice for the sake of extending the gospel of the Kingdom. This means that we are to accept deprivation, imprisonment, and persecution for the sake of Yeshua. Paul's life is a great example of this.

In addition, all of this is predicated on a change in the ages, for the Kingdom of God has broken into this age. The Hebrew text has to be applied to this transitional age where the Kingdom has broken into this world. The central concern of the New Covenant Scriptures is to extend the Kingdom of God to the nations and to disciple all peoples. This requires material support. **Therefore the idea of people storing up wealth for opulent living is never supported as an option in the New Covenant Scriptures.** Therefore we now answer the questions at the beginning of the book.

1. Just what is the promise of prosperity in this new covenant period? The promise can be summarized as: God will abundantly supply all your needs for whatever He has called you to do. This abundant provision should not be defined as a standard of opulent living.

2. The next and very important question is what are the conditions for appropriating the promise of prosperity according to today's

new covenant order? The conditions are covenant faithfulness where God and Yeshua are our all in all. In addition, it is a generous heart that gives generously. The faith teachers are correct that this type of generosity and faith require a change in us. That change comes from meditating on and confessing the truths of the Word of God, especially the promises. As Romans 10:17 says, "Faith comes from hearing, and hearing by the word of God." This faith-building pattern is not only for the salvation experience. This confession for abundant provision should not be mechanical but in a context of loving God and affirming an aspect of His character. In addition, corresponding action is necessary to complete faith; and in this case, it is the act of actual giving. Faith giving goes beyond mere calculation and its meager level of generosity. Giving is the seed for the multiplication of wealth or prosperity.

3. What are the principles for spending money or using wealth in the new covenant order, both for those who live by preaching and teaching the Word and those in other professions? Generally, one is to use money for the sake of others and to extend the Kingdom of God. Extending the Kingdom includes bringing God's order or rule to every sphere of existence, business, education, art, science, communication, and the work of the sphere of the body of believers. The standard for the

use of money for personal living is modesty, especially for ministers who are paid for their ministry. We will expand the meaning of this in the next chapter.

Chapter 6

CONTEMPORARY APPLICATIONS

THE BIBLE WAS written in the time when economies were based on agriculture. This was the worldwide situation. There were crafts: pottery, sandal making, furniture, lamps, and more. Mining included precious gems, gold, and silver. Trade included gold, silver, spices, and craft articles.

With the industrial revolution, a battle has been joined between those who want to manage economic activity by centralized socialism and others who favor capitalism. Jewish and Christian writers have appealed to the Bible for these economic philosophies! So in making applications, I want to first develop a broader framework.

First of all, we should come to the issues of wealth and poverty from a new covenant perspective. We live in the age of the "breaking in of the Kingdom of God," the "already but not yet Kingdom." The New Covenant Scriptures do not explicitly teach much on the issue of the culture formation institutions of human life. This includes modern business corporations, media and communications, education, entertainment, and science. There is teaching on the family and submission to political leaders. The political philosophy of the New Covenant Scriptures is simply that rulers are responsible for enforcing standards of righteousness and justice. The Hebrew Scriptures provide us with the ideal of a society that is conformed to the will of God. It contains much more information on culture formation and the idea of an ideal society.

An adequate philosophy of the Kingdom of God and its application today requires a joining of the Hebrew Scriptures through new covenant application. In this regard, the prayer of Yeshua, for **God's Kingdom to come and His will to be done on earth as it is in heaven** (Matt. 6:10), cannot be limited to a private personal sphere or merely a religious sphere. Some are speaking of this today in terms of the seven mountains of society and culture formation. These include media, arts and entertainment, politics, education-science, business, family, and the religious mountain. Of course the seven mountains are somewhat of an artificial but useful construct. Reformed theology spoke of such mountains as authority spheres of human existence. Reformed thinkers also give a corrective to the contemporary teaching on the seven spheres noting that the primary sphere is the Church since it is the discipleship center for understanding the basic principles for all spheres. In addition, the family that raises children and the political sphere that sets the laws for sphere operation have a primacy that is not the case with the other four. In Reformed thought, **we are to work to see every aspect of life come into conformity to the principles of God.** We do not know when our Lord will return. We are to occupy until He comes and show the meaning of the Kingdom in every sphere to the fullest extent possible. Since the first century period mostly reflects the period of initial evangelism and establishing congregations, there is little development of the theme of bringing society into conformity to the principles of God's righteousness (Kingdom).

However, it is our conviction that Yeshua's disciples are to be an influence on the society toward righteousness in every sphere of human life. This includes the environment of the earth. This is an implication of calling to be salt and light (Matt. 5:13–17).

When we speak of wealth and poverty, we have to ask the question of biblical justice. Biblical justice is not socialistic leveling. **Rather, righteousness or justice is that order where every person can fulfill their God intended destiny.** It is an order that embraces the truth that every human being is created in the image of God. The order that maximizes human dignity and fulfillment is the order that most reflects Kingdom values and is to be sought by Yeshua's followers. Seeking first the Kingdom is to seek Him (Matt. 6:33), to seek to spread the gospel and to disciple, and to seek to establish His righteous order in the seven mountains or authority spheres of human existence.

This is not a book on economic systems, but I need to touch on this as an introduction to the application of our teaching on wealth. This is because I believe that when a godly person makes lots of money it can be a very good thing. Some are called to create and gather great wealth for the sake of Kingdom advance. To develop this section, I want to speak about capitalism since that is the greatest system of wealth creation.

A. Capitalism and Biblical Faith

Why am I writing this section? It is to provide a basic orientation for people called to business and to foster a good attitude among those are not in business leadership. It is very important to note that so much of our Kingdom advance depends upon the wealth creation of business. This includes financing the spread of the gospel, media, entertainment, educational influence, and humanitarian efforts. A positive attitude to business and business people is crucial. I repent of my attitude in college and graduate school when I looked down on business people.

As a young philosophy teacher, I wanted to have a basic grasp of economic theory. For a season I was a socialist. I studied Marxism and the liberal semi-socialism of John Kenneth Gailbraith (Harvard) and then read some of Milton Friedman's work. Later I read books which I now consider the most profound. First the writings of Thomas Sowell, especially *Race and Culture*,[1] George Gilder's *Wealth and Poverty*,[2] Myron Magnet's *The Dream and the Nightmare*,[3] and finally the greatest defense of capitalism ever written, Michael Novak's *The Spirit of Democratic Capitalism*.[4] Novak is a Roman Catholic whose book turned the Vatican away from a socialistic orientation during the time of John Paul II to a regulated capitalism. In addition, for a history of capitalism the famous sociologist Rodney Stark in *The Victory of Reason*[5] provides us with a book of breathtaking power. Most recently George Gilder's *The Israel Test*[6] confirms the thrust of these books. All of these books support the following conclusions:

First, modern capitalism is a system of economics that delivers humanity from a zero sum game approach to wealth. Instead, human invention and creativity through capitalist financing alone has the potential to lift vast numbers of people out of poverty. Human creativity is based on people being created in the image of God (Gen. 1:26–27), and it is creativity, venturing forth, and the faith of risk taking, which are keys to overcoming poverty.

Stark points out that capitalism first developed in the monastery and was based on the idea that God created a rational universe where we could discover its laws and apply this understanding in invention and trade to better humankind. The writing of Adam Smith some centuries later (eighteenth) on markets, trade, and wealth became a classic statement on this.[7]

Novak and Gilder are not speaking of an unregulated capitalism. Unregulated capitalism tends to stifle competition so that the strong create monopolies that stifle innovation and creative invention. The government is needed to prevent monopolies and to ensure fair competition. In fair competition the best products and services will dominate markets and benefit many people. In modern corporate financing and invention, there is potential for products and services to provide great wealth for the inventor, the investor, and for many employees. In addition, the whole society can benefit. Such benefits in food production, computer advancement, and medical progress are stunning and would never have been developed in socialistic societies. It has been proved over and over again that capitalism and liberty present opportunity whereby creativity is rewarded. When creative product is brought to market and demand follows, the result is great wealth creation. Socialism stifles wealth creation. Central planning over the long run can never make the myriad decisions necessary to sort out what can really add to human life and what will produce economic advance. There must be much trial and error. Only the market can do this.

However, the greatest danger to capitalism is **crony capitalism.** In crony capitalism, the fox is guarding the henhouse. The government favors corporations and protects them from fair competition because of political contributions or other unsavory connections. This increases costs and stifles wealth creation. Some examples of this are how energy inventions were stifled by big oil corporations and car corporations because they would negatively affect their domination in the market. The United States has just gone through a terrible battle over healthcare. I have been very disappointed by the nature of the debate. The whole health system is one of the greatest examples of crony capitalism. It includes insurance companies that have legal protection against our anti-monopoly laws. It includes drug companies who, in league with the government, stifle research testing for natural cures. They cannot make money on natural cures because they cannot patent natural substances. Billions are at stake. Scientific testing is not fostered, and such substances are not brought to market.

This is especially noted by the prominent New York doctor Erica Schwartz. She battles for the legality of bio-identical hormones that do not cause cancer.[8] In addition, trial lawyers have their place in the health system. Hospitals are not truly competitive. So the battle is often between socialism and crony capitalism and neither are the answer to the health crisis. All doctors who practice alternative medicine are very familiar with this problem. This is a primary but not the only reason for the great increase in medical costs. Alternative medicine, tort reform, and real competition would lower costs in spite of the costs of technological advancement. The idea that socialism will produce a good medical system is also an illusion. The politicians simply ignore the real situation and posture against one another.

Central and South America are great examples of societies that swing between crony capitalism and socialism. Michael Novak has written with great brilliance on this.

The recent banking-investment crisis in the United States is largely attributable to crony capitalism. The government was very involved in setting up a system that would lead to the abuses that are all too well known. This included both Democrats and Republicans.

It takes constant vigilance to prevent crony capitalism. It takes disclosure, laws, and a press that understands and investigates the abuses, which today is not sufficiently happening.

These principles should bring us to recognize that wealth creation is good, but must be practiced within certain parameters and according to certain principles. For a follower of Yeshua in business, there are important added principles. Yeshua's disciples may well be called to business. Novak's great book *Business as a Calling* is a worthy read.[9] Our involvement in business through ownership, investment, or as employees at any level should pass some basic tests. First of all, the business should be offering a product or service that will better human life. Some business activity is borderline. Believers need to give themselves to what is not borderline. Secondly, the businesses and corporations should be honestly run, with disclosure of finances and the highest of accounting practices. In addition, the business should pursue high compensation for employees to the extent it can while remaining competitive. In addition, executive salaries should be within a percent that does not compromise the proportionate value for employees or investors. The recent practices of corporate executives getting golden parachutes of huge sums cannot be defended when employees being are laid off and stockholders losing wealth. Such practices are morally repugnant and should be illegal. Why are they not illegal? Crony capitalism!

Business people who follow principles of integrity are heroic figures and should have the respect of all. Believers are called to demonstrate the Kingdom of God in the business sphere! Business people who have integrity often understand faith better than clergy people. They understand that they constantly have to give, venture forth in faith, and not be tight fisted. This is why so many business books seem to be so spiritual. Such books by Stephen Covey[10] or Jim Collins[11] are examples.

In addition, I want to add the importance of society creating structures that care for the needy, the poor, and the aged in a way that does not destroy their dignity. That means that we do not create an intergenerational underclass. Money thrown at problems does not solve the problems. **Personal investment alone can solve systematic poverty.** The culture has to be changed and this often requires religious commitment and change.

B. Modesty as a Biblical Standard

Modesty is not a mathematically precise concept. It is relative to the society in which we live. The issue of modesty answers a question for both business leaders, investors, and those who are paid by gospel ministry; namely, how shall we live with regard to wealth? Even with standards of integrity in a business, it is possible for business leaders to accumulate fabulous wealth. This can be done with a very small percentage of the profit of a firm so that there is little change in the wealth benefits to employees and investors. When a business leader accumulates such wealth, how should he or she live? We will address this.

Most ministers of the gospel do live with great modesty. Their compensation packages are often sadly meager. **If one studies the level of compensation of ministers in all denominations and streams of the body of believers, one will find that any claim that most ministers are in it**

for the money are ludicrous. Few are paid as they should be. Poverty or lack among ministers is the overwhelming reality; though, due to media and the abuse of a relative few, we think that financial abuse is common among ministers. It is not! Keeping ministers poor and humble is all too dominant an attitude in the society. Unless one has a call to live totally by faith from day to day, compensation needs to be increased for most ministers! However, we should also note that some relatively few ministers such as television ministers, including their royalties from religious books, and even some with the talent to build very big mega churches have the potential of fabulous compensation packages.

So let us define modesty as a standard for ministers and a challenge for all believers including business leaders. It is modesty for a Western society, not for India or China.

Modesty is a standard of life where the person is able to do the following.

1. Live in a good house in the neighborhood of the people to whom one is called to minister. The standard of life of the people in one's congregation is partly a factor in weighing this. This does not include the idea that one is called to minister to the rich and must therefore live like the rich. If there is a call to the rich, there is certainly a middle class neighborhood nearby that is sufficient!

2. Be able to provide good and healthy food for one's family. Health insurance is also a part of providing.

3. Be able to save for the education of one's children and thus provide for a college education at a basic level. This does not mean that Harvard is fully paid.

4. Be able to save for emergencies and an adequate retirement so one is not an undue burden on the community of faith and to one's children.

5. I would add an adequate recreation and vacation to get away with one's family and to enjoy family fellowship without the pressures of work.

When a paid minister of the gospel goes much beyond this standard, he discredits the gospel in his society. Yes, a minister may have a following that is happy to give to make him rich, but the larger effect is to discredit the gospel and the ministry as a fraudulent scheme. The total testimony to the unbelievers is terribly damaged. Paul warns against the minister getting rich off the gospel. This is why royalties for spiritual books, compensation packages, and honoraria need to be kept within the bounds of modest compensation. In our ministry, our leaders donate their royalties to the ministry for further Kingdom advance. The size of the ministry one leads may have some effect leading to larger compensation, but it should not be that different than the basic modesty standard.

I know the argument of big ministry leaders. They argue that their role is parallel to corporate leaders in the business world. They argue that they could make much more money in that world (maybe). However, none of this is important. Making money is not the passion of those paid for gospel ministry. Rather they are passionate about extending the Kingdom and want to take out as little money as needed for a modest compensation so that the Kingdom may be further extended. They are to be diligent to not discredit the gospel and to not violate Paul's example to not profit off the gospel and to not teach that godliness is a means of selfish financial gain. The ministry can be rich and invest more and more in gospel extension; the minister should not be, unless his wealth comes from business endeavors outside of the gospel ministry. If this is the case, disclosure should show a strict separation of compensation, and perhaps a wealthy person can serve at no cost. An Alaskan minister, Dick Benjamin, taught people to go into business and to do well, and then serve the community of faith for free. Benjamin led the Abbot Loop Church and fellowship of churches and was one of most prominent of teachers on the fivefold ministry in the last generation.

I want to emphasize again that the greatest problem of money in ministry is believing for prosperity to extend the Kingdom and adequately paying ministers. Those who abuse prosperity teaching or who teach a false doctrine of prosperity sadly have caused a reaction which has undercut our ability for ministers and ministries to escape the poverty mentality. This is because the abuses have caused people to not see the legitimacy of a true faith prosperity message and generous but modest compensation for ministers a goal.

Ministries should generally follow the standards of disclosure and accounting of the Evangelical Council of Financial Accountability whether or not they are formal members. This great organization has been a key to raising the issues of integrity. I believe that financial disclosure is a key guard for the reputation of the body of believers and ministers of the gospel. Members of congregations and donors to ministries should know where the money is being spent. Financial statements should be available. In addition, the compensation packages for full-time ministers should be disclosed. This was an historic standard in historic Protestant denominations. The independent congregations and ministries that have strayed from this wise standard have taken a direction that more readily enables abuse. Yes, there might be a board of elders or a compensation committee that sees that such compensation packages meet the standard put forth here. They may also fear the criticism of small-minded people who will be envious of the provision given to the minister. However, such compensation teams sometimes become like an "old boys'" network, as we see in some corporate boards. In addition, it is worthy to put up with some carping from the immature. This is because of the greater testimony of openness. One realizes the blessing of this standard over the years. Of all the financial scandals that have been reported in the secular press over the years discrediting the gospel in to the unbelieving world, one can hardly find such scandals in the historic denominations. Why? Because they have a tradition of integrity in managing funds, systems of accountability, and disclosure that go a long way in protecting the body of the Messiah.

However, what should be the standard for believers who are business leaders or leaders in other sectors of society, sports stars, media personalities, and others who can accumulate great wealth?

The basic issue for such leaders is to use their gain for Kingdom expansion. This Kingdom expansion includes the expansion of their business. Successful businesses are able to also support humanitarian work through corporate charity. This is part of our law system in America and in other countries.

However, what about the use of compensation from large corporations that can be very large indeed for business executives? The standard of modesty is also relevant for such corporate leaders. While the corporation may pay handsomely according to the going rate for such leaders, the question of what to do with the compensation still looms. Modesty is not as exacting, in my view, for business leaders or others who receive great levels of compensation in the business world. They did not get paid for the ministry, so this does not discredit the gospel. Here are some principles.

1. Business leaders know that sowing gain into expansion is a faith matter that brings greater gain and that hoarding wealth is not good behavior. It leads to business decline.

2. Those with significant wealth act contrary to the claims of the Kingdom if they are not seeking make the major emphasis of their lives to primarily use their personal wealth for the extension of the Kingdom of God that can be expressed in all spheres or the seven mountains.

3. There is also liberty in the Spirit. We cannot preclude the Spirit of God giving wealthy leaders a sense that He wants to bless them with some extravagant gifts. God can offer a yacht, a mansion, or other gifts to such people. These gifts are received and known

by the inner man to be something God is offering. We should not reject such a possibility as long as the wealthy leader uses his wealth primarily for the Kingdom. In addition, most wealthy individuals who sense God's favor for such gifts use them to bless others too. We have had board meetings on yachts and know of one business person who uses a mansion as a center for meetings for the Kingdom of God. How many pastors, non-profit gatherings, and weddings have been held on his property at little or no cost! This is acceptable because God is not limited. It is a false idea to think that because a business man has bought an expensive car, souls will die who would otherwise have heard the gospel. This is zero sum thinking. As long as it is really God giving a gift and not covetousness, God will be multiplying wealth and Kingdom advance for the Kingdom. God is not so limited as to not be able to give him a gift. The walk in the Spirit is the key.

4. However, having given qualification concerning God giving personal rewards to a business leader, sports celebrity, or media-entertainment figure, the standard of modesty still applies. Flaunting opulence is never appropriate, and projecting modesty even for rich people is to be valued. Indeed, this is a corollary of a true heart that wants to give to the fullest extent possible to extend the Kingdom of God.

In regard to this point, I am touched by the leader of Spectrum Financial, Ralph J. Doudera, who is a major financial supporter of Haggai Leadership Ministries. In his book *Business as a Calling*, he gives an example of his love for racing cars and his wrestling with God as to whether He really wants to bless him with such a car. This shows the right attitude. He does not assume it or covet it in a wrong way, but in his walk with God, he asks. And yes, with humility he received the car. It is a wonderful book featuring a businessman of integrity who seeks to use his wealth for the Kingdom![12]

One of the really important gifts of our society for wealthy individuals is the legal right to start foundations. This is a very good way to not lay up treasures on earth but to invest funds for the Kingdom. It is not usually wise to give everything away! Good investments can have much greater long-term impact in financing Kingdom expansion. There are many different kinds of charitable trusts as well. Some are family run and some have boards who allocate funds according to specifically defined purposes and goals. In this way finances can increase and enable greater Kingdom effectiveness. The idea is to make the charitable foundation wealthy and not the individual.

THE CONCLUSION OF THE MATTER

Therefore, the conclusion of the matter is that God wills all to prosper, but in the context of His calling, whether to prosper in having His strength in prison, beatings, and persecution to a faith stand to see God provide day to day. The call of George Mueller, who provided for thousands of orphans and never accumulated wealth, is still a great example of prosperity to which some are called.[13] The similar faith orientation of a Hudson Taylor is still a great model.[14] LeTourneau gave away 90 percent of his income and became wealthy on the 10 percent.[15] We have today's great example of Heidi Baker in Mozambique who like George Mueller has provided for thousands of orphans.[16]

Many ministers are called to receive more ordinary compensation as they live by preaching and teaching the Word. Some business people are called to produce great gain for the sake of Kingdom expansion. There is no new covenant promise to live in opulent wealth, as if as King's children we should all live like Kings. We have to get the promise right before confessing and believing the promise. That promise is abundant provision, not opulent living. In the new covenant period, our priority is Kingdom expansion, not personal opulent living. We have to get it right. God's promise can generally be summed up as: **God will abundantly provide whatever you need for whatever He has called you to do.**

This we can confess; this we can stand upon. It is God's promise to those who live wholeheartedly for Him.

Addendum: What about Cathedrals?

In the New Testament period, the basic gathering of the body of believers was in the house. The emphasis on larger gatherings as a replacement is wrong. Many large buildings in the evangelical world become white elephants in the next generation. Yet, some have been led by the Spirit to build and have had great supernatural confirmation to do so. There is also the history of great synagogue buildings and soaring cathedrals. There have always been those who have asked as to whether or not such funds could have been given to minister to the poor. Again, this could be zero sum thinking.

This is a difficult question. First of all, gathering in larger settings for great preaching and worship is legitimate. God can lead some to build buildings and has. In addition, great cathedrals and synagogues have been a source of inspiration for so many. These inspiring architectural gems are palaces for the poor, who get to enjoy the setting they would never be able to enjoy in king's palaces. A small amount per person builds a large building. God is not limited in funds. Overall, the percentages in world wealth use are small. I would only say that a building should not be the spending center for people, but this should be the ministry of preaching, teaching, evangelism, and discipleship. However, on the issue of buildings, we look at the ancient Temple of Solomon and realize that for a nation of a few million, this was quite an undertaking. In the same way centers in cities are a focus of spiritual meaning. It is according to God's leading and confirmation.

PART II

INVESTING AND FOSTERING
WEALTH CREATION

Chapter 7

RESPONSIBLE INVESTING IN
ACCORD WITH BIBLICAL VALUES

I BELIEVE IT IS worthwhile to present a biblical perspective on investing. I believe that unless one has a special calling to live by faith on a day-to-day basis or a special word from God to have no savings, that the normative orientation for most people should be to save and invest in such a way that one provides adequately for the future. We defined adequate provision in earlier chapters. It included that we are to provide good food and shelter for our families. We also are responsible for the education of our children and income for our senior years, including basic health care. This can only be accomplished if there is savings and investment to grow wealth.

There are people who argue against personal investing, savings, and growing personal wealth sufficient to provide for oneself and one's family in the future. Texts that tell us to not worry about tomorrow or to lay up treasure on earth are used to undercut what we are going to say in this chapter (Matt. 6:34, 19). In addition, Yeshua's counsel for the rich man to sell everything and follow Him is universalized (Mark 10:21; Matt. 19:21). I do not think this is the biblical orientation. It contradicts the Torah and much of the counsel in Proverbs as well as the example of the Patriarchs. I think instead that the New Covenant

Scriptures are attacking greed and hoarding. Hoarding is contrary to the right heart in an investor.

As I write these words, the American economy is in a difficult time of recession. Successful investing with integrity requires a system of government enforcement of fair competition and regulation that provides a fair and just compensation for those who invest. Even apparently good investments can turn sour if the financial management of the country is bad or the trend for markets is in serious decline. So everyone who invests needs to take such factors into consideration. My comments will be for normal conditions where there is a reasonably just order.

Love should be the motivation for our investing. What is love? I came to the following definition through a thorough study of the Bible. Love is the compassionate identification with others that motivates us to seek their good. Their good is defined by their fulfilling the good destiny that God has for them. Love must be guided by the Law of God and is consistent with this Law. A loving investor wants to invest not only to provide for their own prosperity but to be able to expand businesses and services that improve the lives of others. **Investing is business-wealth creation participation.** In addition, if one is called to it, investing can produce a larger increase whereby the investor is able to give more to benefit others.

The most basic investment of the most ethical kind is what Warren Buffet has come to typify as value investing. Value investing is investing in a good company that one believes in for the long term. In value investing, one studies the company and its product or service, its management, and what others who are experts and have a good track record say about the company. In addition, we should look at the product and ask if it is something that enhances human life. Such investing expands the economy and wealth is created that benefits all sectors of society. I believe that this is the highest level of ethical business investment.

Such investment contrasts with hoarding where one puts money in gold or diamonds because they will appreciate. They may appreciate, but unless one ultimately sells and invests it will not expand wealth for the society. I am not saying that one should not own gold and silver for emergencies and economic upheaval but that owning the metal itself does little to benefit others. I do not object to investing in commodity stock including gold, silver, other metals, as well as energy stock, since these resources are needed in all kinds of industrial applications to expand our economy.

One can also see other distortions in investing such as in the last real estate bubble. Many investors bought houses to flip them and pocket the profit. This was part of running up a housing bubble, the popping of which produced a terrible loss for many people. The idea that housing would always rise was a wrong idea. Houses should be bought primarily to provide shelter or to rent as a good service to others who cannot afford or prefer not to buy. When a house is paid off, the house can legitimately be sold and the funds can provide for one's old age, but the house alone is not sufficient in most circumstances to provide for the future.

The reader can conclude that I am negative to speculative investing. While trends do need to be taken into account, I am negative to investing that simply seeks to ride market trends and buy low and sell high without regard to the product or service. The motive is merely to make money and not to invest in ways that better society.

Of course, trends are part of investment growth and have to be taken into account, but only as one consideration. There are all kinds of approaches to investing that turn the stock market into something of a gambling casino. I am speaking here of option trading which can be very lucrative. One can trade on the basis that a company will decline and bet on that decline and make a great amount of money. We as believers would be then exercising a negative faith against a company as a way to make money. The gambling dimension of markets is troubling, and I have sometimes wondered if investing should be limited to purchasing into a company and having to hold it for a reasonable period of at least some weeks or months.

In addition, there are many investments that do quite well that no Kingdom oriented believer can embrace. One newsletter recommends a sin portfolio—pornography, tobacco, and gambling. Do I have to say that this is not an option for a follower of Jesus? The products destroy life!

On this basic basis I now will sort some kinds of investments and evaluate them.

I. Basic stock investments.

The philosophy of value investing in a good company with a good product or service for the long term should normally be the investment strategy of those who have the time, knowledge, and energy to handle their own investing. The result of such investing during most of the twentieth century has been that the company is able to expand and increase its sales, the people who buy the product or service benefit, and the investor gets a good return on his investment and increases his or her personal wealth. Investing is itself a decision of faith. One has to decide between companies that are established and have a solid track record and a good prospect for future growth over against newer companies and products where the risk is greater and both the return and loss potential are greater. Most investment counselors advise a portfolio with large stable companies (blue chips) and some riskier companies. Then there is the challenge of investing in domestic companies and foreign companies which may be more speculative, but foreign companies are not always riskier.

For most people, the challenge of designing one's own portfolio is too much. Therefore they should pick an investment counselor who will discuss investment goals with the investor and will recommend a balanced portfolio of both risky and safe investments. In a balanced portfolio some stocks will go down and some will go up, but the idea is that the overall portfolio will show significant progress.

My view is that most people should have an investment counselor who is committed to biblical values. Such people will not invest in morally questionable companies. There are several such companies; two of the best are Spectrum Financial and Cornerstone Investments. Committed disciples of Jesus lead both.

II. Stock Funds

Stock funds are one of the better ways for ordinary investors to give into the expansion of the economy and to benefit personally. There are all kinds of funds. Be careful, however, since some funds do include stocks in companies whose products do not meet the biblical moral test. The two companies mentioned above do have funds that explicitly seek to meet this test. If one has sufficient funds, one can invest in Berkshire Hathaway, Warren Buffet's investment fund. One should again look at the specifics in case there are companies one would not want to own. Investors in his fund have done very well.

Index funds invest in a very large number of stocks that reflect the one of the stock indexes such as the Dow Jones or the Standard & Poor's. I think such funds are problematic since they include morally questionable stocks.

There are large cap funds meaning large capitalization and investment in very large companies. There are mid cap and small cap funds. Sometimes these smaller companies do very well and with sufficient study can be shown to be quite solid. However, the key is the fund manager who picks companies that are well vetted and whose prospects in the economy are good. There is even a fund that emphasizes investments consistent with Orthodox Judaism.

There are also funds that emphasize foreign investment. International investing is usually considered important for inclusion in a portfolio. It is part of diversification.

There are many funds that emphasize a particular sector of the economy: energy funds, commodities funds, mining funds, gold funds, health funds (national hospital companies and drug companies), and so many more.

The sheer number of such funds can be quite bewildering. However, a good investment counselor can sort through such information and can recommend a few funds for a balanced portfolio. For many people investing in a few different kinds of funds that are well managed and which have an ethical standard for the companies chosen are good choices. Then one would hold some gold or silver for emergencies.

III. Commercial Bonds

Bonds are usually considered to be safer and less volatile than stocks. Basically a bond is a loan to a company.

The company uses the money to expand its business and pays the holder interest on the bond. The bond can be sold to recover the capital. So bonds in very solid companies are usually good investments and pay higher interest than government bonds and bank savings accounts. However, the investor needs to know that the capital worth in bonds can adjust and are interest rate sensitive. When interest rates in the economy go up, the value of the bond goes down since it is paying less than the going rate and the compensation is to lessen the worth of the bond. When interest rates decline the value of the bond goes up. A bond held to term may be guaranteed to return full capital at maturity. A good investment counselor can help you decide if and what commercial bonds to include. There are commercial bond funds where the fund invests in bonds for the people that invest in the fund. The main danger in bonds is the bankruptcy of a company that by the court proceedings may only pay a fraction back to the bond-holder. The ethical standard for investment is to only lend money to a good company that is providing a good service or product to people. The company should measure up to the same standards for management and growth.

IV. Municipal Bonds (State Bonds)

Municipal bonds, called *munis*, have been a very solid investment and guaranteed to return full capital. The interest payments are higher than many other bond instruments. However, we are living in day when these very safe investments are not as certain as in the past. Why? Because of overspending by state and municipal governments. There are also commitments to public employees for high pensions and benefits that cannot be sustained. So the investor should search for bonds where the city or state is well managed with commitments that can be covered by the tax base. The advantage of municipal bonds is that the income is deductible from income taxes, so it is tax free income! On an ethical basis, municipal bonds help states provide for education, infrastructure, and more that is important for states and cities. However, the ethical standard for investing should lead to only investing in well managed cities or states.

V. Savings Accounts

Savings accounts are almost the equivalent of the biblical parable of burying the talent of gold in the ground. The interest rates have been very low, below the rate of inflation. Investments in banks savings accounts do provide money that expands banking reserves that enable the bank to give more loans for business expansion. This is good. The bank may not have the same ethical standards for its loans as the disciple would have for his personal investing. The present state of return makes this a poor investment. A minimum amount in savings accounts providing for free checking, safety deposit box services, etc., does make a basic savings account worthwhile.

We should note that many of the services provided by banks, including credit cards, checking, and savings, can be done through credit unions that usually give a better deal than the banks. Investment companies also can provide some of these services.

VI. Treasury Bonds, Government Savings Bonds

Through much of the twentieth century, treasury bonds have been considered the very safest of investments since they are backed by the full faith and credit of the U. S. government. They have been traditionally used to guarantee capital. The interest rates are presently low and barely keep up with inflation. Only recently with the great increase of U. S. debt has the reality of a U. S. default become a possibility. Probably the government would avoid default by printing money and inflating the currency. Treasury bonds can be bought for different terms, for six months (a treasury bill) to several years. The longer term bonds bring the risk of interest sensitive bonds in general and the capital can increase or decrease. If the bond is held to maturity, however, the full face value is paid. The issue, however, is that the interest rates may be such that holding the bond may turn out to be a bad investment. However, for capital preservation, treasuries can still be included in a portfolio. What about the ethical standards for investment? Investing in the U. S. government would seem to pass the ethical test since it finances all kinds of government programs and projects. However, if one has concerns with government overspending and one believes that many government programs are not to the benefit of the citizens, then one would question treasury investments. An investment counselor can give current information in treasuries.

VII. Mortgage Bonds

One can invest in two semi-private companies that provide mortgages and back mortgages; one is called Fanny Mae and the other Freddy Mac. These instruments paid slightly below the rate of return on mortgages. They were considered very safe investments with reasonable return. Today, there are several issues with investing in these instruments. For one thing, interest rates are very low. In addition, there are great questions about these companies backing sub-prime loans. They have been running great losses and have had to have huge government bailouts. So we would question their use for investments. Backing mortgages in normal times would seem to pass our ethical test in providing a service of great value, but the mismanagement from the federal government make this riskier.

VIII. Currency Trading:

A great deal of money can be made by betting on the trends of currency in different nations. The name George Soros comes to mind. In currency trading one seeks to make money on the basis of buying the currency of a foreign country. The currency goes up and then one seeks to sell it when its rise comes to an end. Then one can buy another currency or can purchase dollars. Currency trading does not produce a good or a service of any value. However, one can invest in funds in a foreign company that will track with the currency of that country. This may be a good way to preserve one's wealth while advancing goods and services that are of value in the chosen country.

IX. Annuities

There are all kinds of annuities. These instruments work by the individual giving a corporation funds in return for a fixed return of income. Some annuities have a payout to the investor or heirs and others keep the capital for the organization. For example, one can give an annuity to a Christian college in return for an agreed upon income for life in return for the organization keeping the capital after the person dies. Insurance companies also offer annuities that also have a payout to heirs. Generally annuities can be a very good way of stewardship if one supports the organization that will benefit. The ethical value of supporting a Christian college or another organization that benefits the public is very good. One should again consult a good investment counselor on using annuities.

X. Retirement Planning

The U. S. government makes tax deferred investment programs and tax advantaged investments a very positive opportunity for retirement planning. We list and describe several here. We again note that the investments from these programs should pass the ethical standards we have outlined here.

A. IRAs stands for Individual Retirement Accounts. These are investment accounts available through brokerages that defer federal taxes for all funds contributed. At the present time each individual can contribute up to $5,000.00 per year. Over the course of thirty or even forty years, this can build quite a large retirement if invested well. A couple then could, by individual investing, put $10,000 per year into an investment. When one retires they draw from the IRA and pay taxes on the amounts taken. One can contribute to this until the age of seventy-three, but at that age it is a taxable fund and one can only take funds and not contribute. A Roth IRA is a modification established by congress some years ago. With this instrument, one has no tax deduction on the funds invested, but all funds that are invested accrue free interest growth and there is no taxation when the funds are taken upon retirement. In the course of a life of investing, the Roth IRA will produce greater benefits since the non-taxation of the growth and the use after retirement is to one's greater benefit.

B. There are instruments that work like IRA but allow greater amounts of funds to be place in retirement funds with deferred taxation. A SEPT account is the primary example of this for self-employed persons.

C. Keoghs and 401K plans work like IRA but are plans where employers give as part of employee benefits. In these plans the employer gives the funds and the employee can choose among various investment possibilities. In addition, the employee can contribute personal funds to increase the amount available for investment.

D. Reverse mortgages are very good instruments for retired people who do not have sufficient income for their retirement and are willing to give up an inheritance from their house for their children. The bank offers to pay the retired owners of the house an income with interest until the equity in the house is exhausted. The owner can stay in the house as long as they can pay the taxes and insurance for the house. At their death the company, bank, or insurance company owns the house.

E. Charitable Trusts: Wealthy individuals can also support charities by establishing trusts where the interest can support the family while the capital can be designated to the charity. Eventually the fund grows to such an extent that it can actually recover all of the money given. Or the fund can grow and some can be taken to support charities in the interim. There are professionals that specialize in charitable trusts. This is highly recommended as a wonderful way to support charities.

Conclusion:

It is my hope that this summary of investing will be a benefit to the reader. I encourage all to invest with biblical ethics in mind.

NOTES

Introduction
Prosperity and the Torah

1. Yediot Ahronot, "Attitudes Towards Jesus and Christianity," December 24, 2009, *Caspari Media Review*, January 5, 2010, http://caspari.com/media_review/2010/10-01-05.html (accessed March 25, 2016).

2. Ronald Sider, *Rich Christians in an Age of Hunger: Moving from Affluence to Generosity* (Nashville, TN: W. Publishing Group, 1997).

3. K. P. Yohannan, *Come, Let's Reach the World* (Carrollton, TX: GFA Books, 2004).

Chapter 1
Prosperity and the Torah

1. Martin Hengel, *Prosperity and Riches in the Early Church: Aspects of a Social History of Early Christianity* (Philadelphia: Fortress, 1974).

2. Thomas Sowell, *Race and Culture: A World View* (New York: Basic Books, 1994).

3. Annie Johnson Flint, "What God Hath Promised," http://www.hymnary.org/text/god_hath_not_promised_skies_always_blue (accessed March 25, 2016).

Chapter 2
Psalms, Proverbs, and Prophets

1. Tim Holt, "The Kantian Moral Argument," *Philosophy of Religion*, http://www.philosophyofreligion.info/theistic-proofs/the-moral-argument/the-kantian-moral-argument/ (accessed April 2, 2016).

2. Michael L. Brown, *Compassionate God or Consuming Fire?* (Bethesda, MD: Messianic Vision Press, 1985).

Chapter 6
Contemporary Applications

1. Sowell.

2. George F. Gilder, *Wealth & Poverty* (New York: Basic Books, 1981; Richmond, CA: ICS Press, 1993).

3. Myron Magnet, *The Dream and the Nightmare* (New York: William Morrow, 1993).

4. Michael Novak, *The Spirit of Democratic Capitalism* (New York: Simon and Shuster, 1982).

5. Rodney Stark, *The Victory of Reason* (New York: Random House, 2005).

6. George F. Gilder, *The Israel Test* (Minneapolis: Richard Vigilante Books, 2009).

7. Adam Smith, *An Inquiry into the Nature and Causes of Wealth of Nations*, 3 vols. (London: Strahan and Cadell and Davies, 1796).

8. Dr. Erika's website: https://www.drerika.com/.

9. Michael Novak, *Business as a Calling* (New York: The Free Press, 1996).

10. Dr. Stephen Covey's website: https://www.stephencovey.com/.

11. Jim Collin's website: http://www.jimcollins.com/.

12. Ralph J. Doudera, *Wealth Conundrum* (Atlanta, GA: Signature Editions, 2005).

13. "George Mueller, Orphanages Built by Prayer," *Christianity.com*, http://www.christianity.com/church/church-history/church-history-for-kids/george-mueller-orphanages-built-by-prayer-11634869.html (accessed April 4, 2016).

14. Ed Reese, "James Hudson Taylor," *Wholesome Words*, http://www.wholesomewords.org/missions/biotaylor2.html (accessed April 4, 2016).

15. "R.G. LeTourneau—Earthmoving Innovator," *Giants for God*, http://www.giantsforgod.com/rg-letourneau/ (accessed April 4, 2016).

16. Heidi Baker's website: http://www.irisglobal.org/.

ABOUT THE AUTHOR

D R. DANIEL JUSTER received his BA from Wheaton College, his MDiv from McCormick Theological Seminary; did two years in the philosophy of religion program of Trinity Evangelical Divinity School and received his ThD from New Covenant International Seminary. Dr. Juster has been involved in the Messianic Jewish movement since 1972. He was the founding president and general secretary of the Union of Messianic Jewish Congregations for nine years, the senior leader of Beth Messiah Congregation, Rockville, Maryland for twenty-two years, and presently is a member of the apostolic team that governs Tikkun International Ministries. Tikkun International is an umbrella organization for an apostolic network of leaders, congregations, and ministries who share a common commitment; namely the restoration of Israel and the Church. Dr. Juster is also the director of the Tikkun America of congregations; and as such, he provides oversight to some twenty congregations in the USA. He presently ministers personally under the name of Restoration from Zion, a Tikkun ministry.

Tikkun is committed to: (1) training; (2) sending out and supporting congregational planters in the USA, Israel, and other countries; (3) fostering Jewish ministry in local churches; (4) helping to support an international network of Bible and graduate schools for training leaders for the

Jewish vineyard and for work in the rest of the church (presently there are schools in Odessa, Moscow; and Buenos Aires, Argentina, and Zimbabwe).

Dr. Juster has authored several books, including *Jewish Roots, A Foundation of Biblical Theology, The Dynamics of Spiritual Deception, Jewishness and Jesus, The Biblical World View: An Apologetic, Relational Leadership, The Irrevocable Calling, One People, Many Tribes,* and *Mutual Blessing.* He has been involved as a featured speaker at many conferences, both nationally and internationally.

Presently, Dan and his wife, Patty, spend most of their year in Israel near Jerusalem and four months' travel in the United States. He has three married children and eight grandchildren who live in the Israel.

CONTACT

THE AUTHOR

Email: danieljuster@gmail.com